Guide to Capturing a Plum Blossom

Guide to Capturing a Plum Blossom

BY Sung Po-jen

TRANSLATED BY Red Pine

詩 Copper Canyon Press
Port Townsend, Washington

Copper Canyon Press is in residence at Fort Worden State Park in Port
Townsend, Washington, under the auspices of Centrum. Centrum is a
gathering place for artists and creative thinkers from around the world,
students of all ages and backgrounds, and audiences seeking extraordinary
cultural enrichment.

LIBRARY OF CONGRESS CATALOGING-IN-PUBLICATION DATA

Song, Boren.
[Mei hua xi shen pu. English]
Guide to capturing a plum blossom / by Sung Po-jen; translated by
Red Pine.—2nd ed.
    p. cm.
ISBN 978-1-55659-378-9 (alk. paper)
1. Song, Boren.   2. Flowering plums in art.   3. Flowering plums—Poetry.
I. Red Pine, 1943–   II. Title.
ND1049.S795A4 2011
759.951—dc23

                                                            2011030948

Second edition

9 8 7 6 5 4 3 2 FIRST PRINTING

Copper Canyon Press
Post Office Box 271
Port Townsend, Washington 98368
www.coppercanyonpress.org

for Paul Hansen

CONTENTS

PREFACE TO THE REVISED EDITION

This book has been out of print for more than a decade, and a number of readers have asked when it might once again be available. Naturally, it has been my hope to see it back in print, and I have also wanted to revisit my earlier translations and notes. Copper Canyon has now given me the opportunity to fulfill both of these wishes, and I have spent the past few months trying to improve on my efforts of sixteen years ago.

In passing on the results to the reader, I would be remiss if I did not also take this opportunity to direct them to the work of Maggie Bickford. In 1995, the same year the Mercury House edition of this book came out, Professor Bickford published an article discussing Sung Po-jen's work in volume 6 of *Asia Major*'s third series entitled "Stirring the Pot of State: The Southern Sung Picture-Book *Mei-Hua Hsi-Shen P'u* and Its Implications for Yuan Scholar-Painting." Although the article is archived in 1993's volume 6, it was not published until 1995, and I was not able to benefit from its scholarship until now. As far as I know, it remains the only serious effort to address the various issues associated with the production and impact of Sung's book, and I would recommend anyone interested in a more scholarly approach to his *Guide* to consult this article, which is available online at *Asia Major*'s website.

Red Pine
Summer 2011
Port Townsend, Washington

TRANSLATOR'S PREFACE

Plum pictures and plum poems have been on my mind ever since I found Sung Po-jen's *Guide to Capturing a Plum Blossom* in China's old cultural capital of Hangchou, west of Shanghai. That was six years ago, a few days before the tanks rolled through Tienanmen in June of 1989. I was browsing through the only bookstore in Hangchou that sold old books, and I found a hand-bound copy of the 1928 edition of Sung's *Guide* on a shelf with other dusty survivors of the Cultural Revolution. I had never heard of Sung Po-jen or his book, but I was captivated by the pictures. I bought the store's only copy and took it back to my hotel room and tried to read the poems. I soon realized that the poetry of a thirteenth-century scholar-official was beyond my reach, which was limited to the more accessible works of Chinese Buddhists. I put the book down, and a few weeks later, back in Taiwan, I gave it to my friend Lo Ch'ing. It was a fortuitous decision.

Lo Ch'ing had studied art with the last emperor's cousin, and he had heard of Sung Po-jen's *Guide,* but he had never seen a complete copy. Surprised by our good fortune, we agreed to enjoy the book together. Every Wednesday for the next four months, we sat down on the straw mats in Lo Ch'ing's tea room, surrounded ourselves with piles of dictionaries, dynastic histories, anthologies, and compendia of all sorts, and spent the whole morning working our way through five or six poems and as many pots of tea.

As the result of our joint efforts, I was able to make rough translations into English. But before I had time to polish them sufficiently for publication, I put them aside to finish work on a book about Chinese hermits, then to embark on a series of journeys in China that involved the production of more than a thousand radio programs, and finally to move back to America. It has taken me five years to pick them up again.

I regret the long delay as well as the mistakes I may have made where I have ignored Lo Ch'ing's advice and followed my own perverse interpretations. The notes, too, hardly do justice to our weekly explorations or to the background Sung Po-jen expected of his readers. But the Thundercloud plum I planted last year outside my window has begun to let go of its first blossoms, and I can no longer hold on to these. In passing them on to the reader, I hope that something of their original fragrance has remained and that the pictures, reproduced from the edition of 1261, will make up for any loss of spirit.

Red Pine
Spring 1995
Port Townsend, Washington

INTRODUCTION

Sung Po-jen's *Mei-hua hsi-shen-p'u,* or *Guide to Capturing a Plum Blossom,* was printed from woodblocks in 1238 and thus became the world's earliest-known printed book of art. Two decades later, a copy of the book passed into the hands of the Chinhua Shuangkueitang Publishing House, and the publisher added this short note to his 1261 edition of the book:

> Those who sing the praises of the plum flower might capture its form but not its essence. Recently, I came across this book, which not only succeeds in capturing the flower's spirit but also explores its inexhaustible forms. Reading it is like chewing sugarcane: the longer you chew, the better it tastes. Surely this is the crown of plum flower poetry.

Despite such praise, Sung's book would have been lost if a single copy of the 1261 edition had not come down to us in the following manner:

When the Mongols completed their conquest of China in 1276, the mixture of Chinese nationalism and aesthetics displayed in Sung Po-jen's *Guide* became treasonous, and his book disappeared from public notice. Although artists consulted the book in private, none were willing to affix their names to our surviving copy until it appeared 300 years later in the collection of the sixteenth-century painter Wen Cheng-ming.

After Wen died, his copy passed through other unknown hands for another 200 years, until it surfaced in Peking's antique market, as described by the famous collector and book connoisseur Huang P'i-lieh in the colophon that he added to the book:

> At the beginning of 1801, I decided to travel north with my friends Ku Nan-ya and Hsia Fang-mi. The day we left,

my friend Ch'u Mu-fu presented me with an album of plum flower paintings. I put them in my luggage thinking to ask friends along the way to add their poems on the facing pages. Shortly afterward, my friend Ch'en Chung-yu joined us, and we sailed off together.

After we arrived at Maple Bridge,[1] my relative Yuan T'ing-t'ao came to see us off with wine and presented us with a branch of plum flowers from his garden to wish us good luck in the civil service examination. We took a line from the T'ang poem that goes, "I have nothing to give but a branch of spring," and we all wrote poems with this as our inspiration.

From there we continued on to Yangchou,[2] where Nan-ya painted four plum flower paintings in a snow-storm, one of which depicted Shou-chieh presenting his gift,[3] and all of which we added to Mu-fu's album. Enjoying ourselves, we titled the album "Plum Flower Words Are Perfumed Words."

In the middle of the second month, we finally arrived in Peking and went looking for books in the Liulichang antique market. At the Wentsui Bookstore, I found a Sung dynasty copy of *Guide to Capturing a Plum Blossom*. I was amazed that such a rare treasure would fall into my hands, and at the same time I was reminded of the paintings of Ch'u Mu-fu and Ku Nan-ya. It was such a coincidence, I summoned my old friends, and we met again to write poems about my new treasure.

Later, after I returned home, I failed to find Sung's book listed in the reader's guide to Ch'ien Tseng's famous

---

1. A famous Suchou bridge on the Grand Canal south of the Yangtze.
2. Where the Grand Canal continues north of the Yangtze.
3. Shou-chieh is a sobriquet of Yuan T'ing-t'ao.

collection of books. Fortunately, I had also acquired a later, more complete version of Ch'ien's reader's guide, and here I found Sung's book listed. Finally, I realized what a rare possession my copy of the 1261 edition was.

Recognizing the book's importance, Huang asked his relative Yuan T'ing-t'ao to make two copies in outline form, one of which he presented to the famous scholar Juan Yuan. Juan added his own colophon to this copy and passed it on to the Ch'ing court, where it was reprinted in the collection of books known as the *Yuan-wei pieh-tsang*. Yuan T'ing-t'ao's second tracing was also reprinted, though not until after his death, by the Kuniyuan Publishing House. In addition to spreading the book's fame through these two outline copies, Huang also had the 1261 edition reprinted in its original form in 1823 among the later collections of the Chihputsu Library. I recently came across a copy of this edition, collected earlier by Chou Tso-jen, the brother of Lu Hsun, and added it to my own collection.

In 1851 Huang's own copy of the book passed into the hands of Yu Ch'ang-sui, and Yu loaned the book to the painter Chiang Chung-li, who refused to return it. Only through trickery was Yu able to get the book back, and he added this note to its growing list of colophons: "I will never show this book to anyone who has not been my friend for at least ten years." Yu called it among the most precious objects in the world.

From Yu Ch'ang-sui the book passed to P'an Tsu-yin and then to P'an Ching-shu, who inherited it in 1921 on her thirtieth birthday. P'an Ching-shu was the wife of the famous painter and collector Wu Hu-fan. The couple loved this book so much, they covered its pages with nearly fifty seals designed especially for the purpose. From P'an and Wu, the book then passed into the collection of the Shanghai Museum, which reprinted it in 1981 and thus made the world's oldest-known printed book of art available for a new and wider audience.

About the book's author, we know next to nothing. According to the brief biography included in Huang P'i-lieh's colophon, Sung Po-jen was a native of the Huchou area of Chekiang province. His sobriquet was Ch'i-chih, and his pen name was Hsueh-yen, both of which had patriotic echoes in Chinese. After passing the poetry section of the civil service examination, he was appointed to supervise the salt trade in Huaiyang along the Grand Canal.[4] This is all we know of the man, except for the few personal notes he slipped into another collection of ninety-odd poems that survive in the *Ssu-k'u ch'uan-shu*.[5]

Although we have no dates for his birth or death, we know Sung lived in southern China in the first half of the thirteenth century, when the northern part of China was in the hands of the nomadic Jurchens, who were, themselves, about to lose the north to the Mongols. Sung wanted to do something to encourage his countrymen to recover the north, and he expressed his frustration and patriotic feelings in his verse, which he likened to withered leaves teasing the wind and dried-up lotus leaves battered by rain. And so he published his book, with its image of the flower that blooms in the middle of winter and with its poems that recall the glories of China's past. In this, Sung was not alone. During this period, Chinese intellectuals turned to their culture's ancient roots for inspiration and solace in the face of disunion and exile. In painting and poetry, they chose the flowering plum as their symbol.

In his own preface, Sung Po-jen had this to say:

> I am so addicted to plum blossoms that I laid out my garden around them and built a pavilion to view them and published a collection of poems called *The Pure and Fragile* in praise of them. And still I failed to exhaust their

---

4. North of Yangchou.

5. Completed in 1782, at imperial request, this was the largest set of books ever assembled anywhere in the world. It included over two million pages of text.

subtlety, much like my ancestor Sung Ching,[6] who turned to writing about clouds when plum blossoms proved too elusive.

When their flowers are in bloom, my heart is filled with the purest snow, and my body is cloaked beneath moonlight. I never tire of lingering beside a bamboo fence or a thatched hut to smell their stamens, to breathe on their petals and inhale their fragrance and to taste their pollen. I enjoy the sight of plum blossoms whether they are facing up or down or are open or folded.

Detached, refined, and rare, beyond the world of red dust, no different from the Two Gentlemen of Kuchu, the Four Worthies of Shangshan, the Six Eccentrics of Chuhsi, the Eight Immortals of Yinchung, the Nine Sages of Loyang, or the Eighteen Scholars of Yingchou,[7] they float beyond the confines of form and the mundane world of humankind and beyond the rhapsodies written on such flowers as the peach blossom or peony.

Thus, I painted the flower from the unfolding of its buds to the falling of its petals. I painted more than 200 portraits, and after eliminating those that were too staid or too frail, I was left with 100 distinct views. And to each I added an old-style poem and titled the result *Guide to Capturing a Plum Blossom*. Actually, though, it is about capturing the spirit of the plum blossom. And while there are also guides that depict peonies, chrysanthemums, and bamboo, this is not the same kind of guide. I have published it in the hope of sharing it with other lovers of plum flowers.

How, someone might ask, can my devotion of time and effort to such an insignificant task be of any use to the

---

6. Sung Ching (663–737) was the author of a famous ode to plum blossoms.
7. These are the names of famous recluses. The Four Worthies also appear in poem 95 of this *Guide.*

world? Might not these pages end up as lids on someone's jars and jugs? Despite such a possibility, surely there are like-minded people who would enjoy turning a few pages when the flowers are not yet in bloom, people who would prefer to fill their imaginations with the beauty of a single branch on Kushan,[8] or the desolation of Yangchou before spring,[9] people who cannot let a day pass without seeing plum flowers, people who could spend their lives thinking about plum flowers. I have not painted plum flowers for the sake of painting plum flowers. In this, the artistry of Hua-kuang or Yang Pu-chih is quite beyond my ability.[10]

Someone also joked, "When this flower's whiteness and perfume are gone, it can stop the thirst of armies with its red and yellow fruit and blend the perfect soup in the tripod of the state. This book of yours should likewise move loyal and patriotic readers to act the part of generals in the field or ministers at court in straightening their sashes and jade scepters and in bringing peace to the kingdom. But by focusing instead on the aesthetic beauty of a half-hidden tree in a garden after a snowfall or a branch reaching beyond a bamboo fence reflected in the water,[11] you have concerned yourself with frozen verse and forgotten the root while chasing among twigs."

I rose and thanked him: "And that is why I have a poem about tripods and soup at the end of my *Guide*." My friend clapped his hands and laughed: "In that case, your *Guide* is not in vain. It cannot be called insignificant

---

8. Referring to the hermitage belonging to Lin Pu (967–1028) on Hangchou's West Lake.

9. Referring to a plum poem written there by Ho Sun (d. 534).

10. Hua-kuang refers to the Buddhist monk Chung-jen (d. 1123); Yang Pu-chih refers to Yang Wu-chiu (1097–1169).

11. Referring to Lin Pu's famous lines about the plum, and at the same time, criticizing art divorced from the world of social responsibility.

or of no use to the world, and it should be spread as widely as possible so that it might be passed on to future generations."

Fortunately for Sung, his book appeared just as the technology of printing, which began with Buddhist sutras in the ninth century, was extended to works of literature and art in the twelfth and thirteenth centuries. This technological revolution also brought with it a new attitude toward knowledge. Until the Sung dynasty, books were the private possessions of those able to afford laboriously produced handwritten copies. The use of woodblocks and movable type suddenly made knowledge reproducible and available in the marketplace. Ideas that were once the preserve of a small elite were now exchanged as easily as other merchandise.

This marked the second of the three stages through which Chinese culture has passed — the first being the invention of writing, the second being the development of printing, and the third being the introduction of personal computers. With the advent of printing, books were produced in great numbers, and private collectors emerged. Intellectuals now had easy access to a wide range of materials on Confucianism, Taoism, and Buddhism that was beyond any one person's capacity to memorize. And the publishing centers that developed provided a fertile ground for a new synthesis of ideas that resulted in what scholars have called neo-Confucianism.

Turning their backs on the traditional approach to the derivation of knowledge from discursive thought, neo-Confucians held that the secrets of Nature could be discovered only through the investigation of things. Painters, too, followed this early scientific approach. And they developed a complicated grammar of painting, as they tried to represent natural forms and landscapes in a seemingly realistic manner.

Realism, though, was not what the Sung painters were after. They were after the essence of things. The great poet and calligrapher Su Tung-p'o (1037–1101) warned his colleagues, however, against a one-sided search for this essence. He held up the works of Wang Wei (701–761), whose paintings, he said, contained poems and whose poems contained paintings, as examples of a more balanced approach. Su maintained that the ultimate goal of both painting and poetry was to express one's feelings and ideas. The creation of a likeness or a verbal cliché was not the goal of art. The goal was to express meaning beyond words and feeling beyond representations, and thus to encourage painters to paint like poets and poets to write like painters.

From the late Northern Sung (960–1127) to the Southern Sung (1127–1276), we begin to see scattered examples of this effort to combine poetry and painting, in which a poem is not merely an annotation to a painting and a painting is not simply an illustration of a poem. Though they might overlap, poetry and painting were seen as each maintaining its own integrity. In this respect, Sung Po-jen's book was the first—and the last—attempt to put Su Tung-p'o's theory into practice on a large scale. It was not only the world's first printed book of art but also the first printed book that combined images and poetry.

Sung's book is also significant because it attempts to fathom the essence of a material object through detailed, empirical examination and uses the results of that examination to form the basis for that object's deconstruction and reconstruction on a different plane. Once readers have the flower's 100 stages memorized, they have the key to the plum flower and the key to Nature as well. With this key they can create their own plum flower universe without having to observe Nature at all. Later painters who wanted to paint plum flowers were encouraged to follow the book rather than Nature. How, they asked, could anyone hope to observe the plum flower as meticulously as Sung Po-jen? This, then, was also the first example of postmodernism in the history of Chinese painting. In Sung's book, form becomes a catalyst for meaning, and conversely, meaning conjures form.

The sudden appearance of this book was unprecedented and represented a climax that has yet to be surpassed. Sung Po-jen's *Guide to Capturing a Plum Blossom* is a most remarkable book indeed, and its flowers are as fresh today as they were over 750 years ago. Breathe in their fragrance and see for yourself.

Lo Ch'ing
April 1995
Taipei, Taiwan

Guide to Capturing a Plum Blossom

Covered Buds
FOUR BRANCHES

麥眼

南枝發岐穎　崆峒占歲登

當思漢光武　一飯能中興

1. Wheat Eyes

a southern branch erupts with buds
unmarked means a year of plenty
Han Kuang-wu comes to mind
restoring the throne with a meal

A southern branch feels the warmth of spring first. The Chinese still look to the plum tree for the first sign of spring, and they examine its buds to predict the coming season of growth. It was from such buds that the career of Emperor Kuang-wu began. The year he was born, nine ears appeared on a single stalk of corn in his district, and his mother named him Hsiu, meaning "grain flower." Later, when he was put in charge of a granary, he sold wheat and millet at discounted prices and gained a large following among the oppressed. In A.D. 25, he toppled the usurper Wang Mang, restored the Han dynasty, and ascended the throne as Emperor Kuang-wu (r. A.D. 25–57). Either Sung wishes his own emperor would follow the lead of Han Kuang-wu and restore the Sung dynasty, or he is calling for someone else to do so. Han Kuang-wu also appears in poem 98, in which his tolerance is noted. Throughout his book, Sung uses such references to show his dissatisfaction with court politics but also to encourage changes in the policies of its leaders, including Emperor Li-tsung (r. 1225–1264). Sung also uses variant forms of characters. In the second line, for example, he uses the name of Mount Kungtung in place of two similar characters that mean "blank" or "unmarked." Puns are also fair game: the Chinese for "meal" is a homophone for "revolution."

柳眼

静看隋堤人　紛紛幾榮辱

蠶腰休逞妍　所見元非俗

2. Willow Eyes

silently watching the Sui Dike procession
the glories and endless failures
willows don't bend to look pretty
but because they see what isn't vulgar

In A.D. 605, Emperor Yang-ti of the Sui dynasty toured the
newly completed Grand Canal in a procession of boats that
stretched for one hundred kilometers. To provide a shaded
promenade and to guard against erosion, the emperor had
willows planted along the dikes. Later, the dynasty's name
was applied to new sections of this important trade route
that linked the Yangtze with the Yellow River. The willow's
hanging catkins remind the Chinese of a woman bending at
the waist, and "willow lane" is a euphemism for a brothel-
lined street. But here, the willows see beyond the vulgar and
behold the transcendent, which is the budding plum blossom,
to which they bow out of respect. A poem by the ninth-
century poet Yuan Chen includes these lines: "Where does
spring appear first / spring appears in the willow eyes."

梅眼

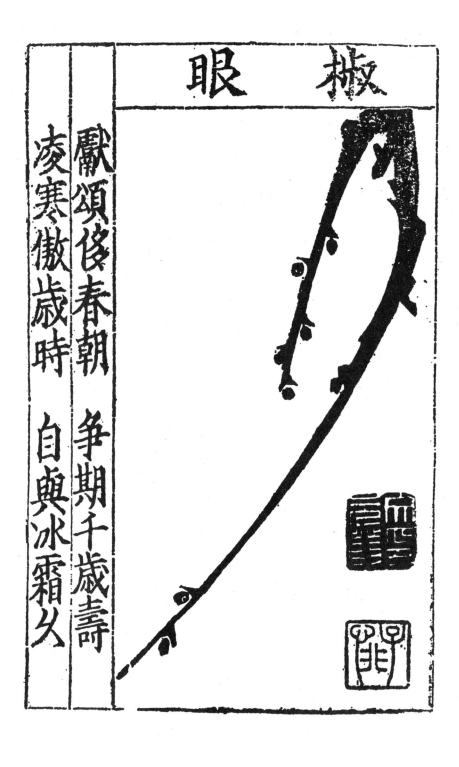

獻頌後春朝　爭期千歳壽
凌寒傲歳時　自與冰霜久

3. Pepper Eyes

lavishing poems on the first spring dawn
prayers for a thousand years
conquering winter and defying old age
outlasting the ice and the snow

Black pepper arrived in China in ancient times as a trade
good from Southeast Asia. Various forms of *huachiao,*
nowadays known as Szechuan pepper, have also been grown
in China for the past 2,000 years. In addition to the use of
pepper as incense to call down ancestral spirits, it was infused
in alcohol to warm the extremities and offered to family elders
on the first day of the new year along with poems wishing
them long life. The Chinese add another year to their ages on
New Year's Day, rather than on their birthdays.

蟹眼

爬沙走江海　慣識風波惡
東君爲主張　顯戮逃砧鑊

4. Crab Eyes

scuttling across sands of rivers and seas
at home in the foulest wind and waves
in the service of the Lord of the East
preferring a public death to the cauldron

When Chinese tea aficionados heat their water, they refer to
the tiny bubbles that first break the surface as "crab eyes," as
the eleventh-century poet Su Tung-p'o did in a poem about
brewing tea: "After the crab eyes, the fish eyes appear." Here,
"rivers and seas" is a metaphor for the world, and "wind and
waves" refers to the vicissitudes of life — and of politics. The
Lord of the East is the spirit of the sun and of spring, but the
phrase also refers to the emperor. In China, crab catchers
traditionally operate at night using torches. The last couplet
suggests this crab would rather die in the service of the
country and even have its body displayed in the marketplace
than accept death in someone's kitchen — referring, I suspect,
to palace intrigue.

Small Buds

SIXTEEN BRANCHES

丁香

小葉一十六枝

藥性貴溫涼　胡爲辛且烈

無與桂附徒　天資更趍熱

5. Cloves

herbs that warm and cool are prized
so why this fire and spice
not following cinnamon's lead
ordained by Heaven to make things hot

Cinnamon is an important ingredient in herbal tonics
designed to revitalize the body without overstimulating it.
As such, its effects are described as both warming and cooling,
and its application in Chinese medicine is extensive. The
major use of cloves is in treating "cold" illnesses that require
something hotter than cinnamon. The Chinese view illness as
an imbalance of yin and yang and treatment as a restoration
of a balance between the two. While reminding the reader of
the beneficial effects of cinnamon, Sung uses the cloves here
to suggest the inflexibility or excess of some policy or person
supported by the emperor.

櫻桃

樊素艷而歌　樂天何所羨

須結帝王知　拜寵明光殿

6. Cherry

Fan-su was lovely and sang
what more could Le-t'ien desire
to gain the emperor's notice
to be favored in the Hall of Light

Of the two girls the ninth-century lyric poet Pai Chu-yi (also known as Pai Le-t'ien) added to his household staff, one of them was Fan-su, whose lips he likened to a cherry. Although Pai served as governor of several important prefectures along the Yangtze, he was sufficiently critical of government policies that he failed to gain the emperor's favor. The Hall of Light was a name for the inner part of the palace, which was lit day and night by the reflections from beaded curtains of gold and jade. Sung obviously sees himself as following in Pai's footsteps and likewise failing to gain his emperor's favor, or even his notice.

老人星

風裂五雲開　明星燦南極
嘉祥自朝廷　何幸愚親識

7. Old Man Star

wind blows apart a rainbow of clouds
a bright star shines due south
auspicious sign for the throne
good fortune for these eyes too

The Old Man Star is Canopus, the second brightest star in the sky after Sirius. It is, however, a southern circumpolar star and only briefly visible in the southern half of China just after the Lunar New Year. Its appearance during the spring festival has caused it to be associated with renewal and long life, and those who see it are said to have an extra year added to their life spans. Since the emperor was acknowledged as the Son of Heaven, all celestial phenomena had a possible bearing on his reign. Not only the presence of certain stars or planets but also the appearance of clouds of certain colors forecast more than the coming weather. The simultaneous appearance of the whole spectrum in the sky was considered the most auspicious of all. The star, of course, refers to the plum blossom, which appears earlier the farther south one goes, and which signals the beginning of another year.

佛頂珠

佛有光明臺 蚌胎奚足貴
聊以孫俗人 徒為寶所費

8. A Buddha's Crown Jewel

buddhas possess a crown of light
more precious than the offspring of oysters
with which they pity poor mortals
wasting their money on jewels

Buddhas are characterized as possessing a number of physi-
cal attributes. A protrusion on the top of the head represents
the attainment of supreme wisdom through meditation.
Despite its radiance, this attribute is only visible to those to
whom buddhas transmit their highest teaching, their crown
jewel. The Chinese once thought pearls were the offspring of
oysters and moonlight. As for who was wasting money on
jewels, Sung is referring not only to people in general but also
to the court and the emperor in particular.

古文錢

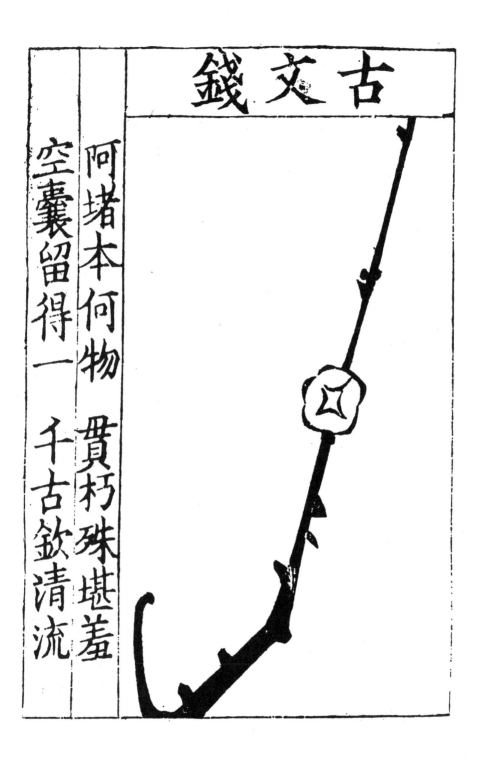

阿堵本何物　貫朽殊堪羞

空囊留得一　千古欽清流

9. Ancient Coin

what the hell is that stuff
rotten cords are shameful
an empty purse still holds something
the ages value honesty

The third-century official Wang Yen was known for his vanity
and pretentious use of language. He was so careful to avoid
the appearance of corruption that he refused to use the word
money and called it "that stuff" instead. To Wang's euphemism
Sung adds another, "what the hell" (*he-wu*) being an expletive
popular in Wang Yen's own day. Until the beginning of the
twentieth century, most Chinese coins had a hole in the
middle that allowed them to be strung together to form larger
denominations. "Rotten cords" suggests unused coins, hence
excessive wealth.

鮑老眉

善舞幾當場　妖姿呈窈窕

當場人自迷　郭郎未容笑

10. Old Pao's Eyebrows

dancing deftly on the stage
seductive yet demure
bewitching all who look
except unsmiling Mister Kuo

Early Chinese drama consisted largely of slapstick sketches involving two characters: a fool and a knave. Among such pairs were Old Pao and Mister Kuo. One of their routines has Kuo dancing and Pao making fun of the length of Kuo's sleeves. When it's Pao's turn, his sleeves turn out to be even longer, eliciting laughter from the audience but disdain from Kuo. Old Pao then outdoes Kuo again with an even greater frown.

兔唇

三窟不須營　淡恬素心友

識盡天下書　只要文章手

11. Rabbit Lips

you don't need to dig three holes
faithful friend of Meng T'ien
you know all the books in the land
let's hope they're better written

A smart rabbit is said to have three holes. Meng T'ien directed
work on the Great Wall in the third century B.C. and is
credited with inventing the Chinese writing brush by tying
rabbit hair to a piece of bamboo. The traditional attribution
notwithstanding, a brush of this description was recently
unearthed in the tomb of a man buried several hundred years
earlier. Until woodblock printing became popular in the
thirteenth century, books were copied out by hand. Too bad,
Sung suggests, so many of them were not worth copying.

虎跡

寒風偃枯草　掉尾來山巔
出柙勢可畏　老鬣寧易編

12. Tiger Tracks

winter wind bends dry grass
flicks its tail along the ridge
a fearful force on the loose
don't try to braid its whiskers

The Chinese liken the north wind that blows down from
Siberia in winter to a roaring tiger. China is home to both
the Siberian and the South China tigers. While both are on the
verge of extinction, the smaller South China tiger still appears
as far north as the Chungnan Mountains south of Sian, where
hermits have shown me their tracks. When Marco Polo visited
China in the thirteenth century, he reported that tigers were
so numerous in the southern parts of the empire that travel-
ing alone was considered dangerous. The tiger was often used
in reference to rapacious officials, but here it most likely refers
to the Mongols, with whom the Southern Sung had joined
forces to defeat the Jurchens in 1234. Thus, the last line would
be a critique of trying to remain on friendly terms with such
a natural enemy.

石榴

錦囊蘊珠璣　長養南風力

當年東老家　曾代中書筆

13. Pomegranate

brocade purse filled with pearls
nourished by a southern wind
long ago old Tung-p'o
used it for a writing brush

The pomegranate was first introduced to China in the second century B.C. from the Central Asian kingdom of Parthia by the Chinese emissary Chang Ch'ien. Since then, the Chinese have used this fruit as a symbol for the womb and its seeds for children. And they compare the south wind that ushers in another cycle of growth in early summer to the kindness parents show their offspring. The eleventh-century poet and calligrapher Su Tung-p'o once visited a hermit and wanted to present the man with a poem. But the hermit was so poor, he didn't have a writing brush. Undeterred, Su used the rind of a pomegranate.

菰　蒱

來自淤泥中　根苗何足取
閟飼上盤登　敢為梨栗伍

14. Arrowhead

growing from the mud and mire
not gathered for its stalk or shoots
placed upon an altar tray
the peer of pears and chestnuts

Arrowhead (*Sagittaria sagittifolia*) is an aquatic plant with
long, arrow-shaped leaves. The white-fleshed tubers that
grow from its roots are eaten and also used for offerings. In
China, white is associated with purity and the spiritual world.
Hence, white-fleshed fruits, including pears and chestnuts,
are considered superior for offerings to ancestors. I can see
Sung wondering why, if even the lowly arrowhead was worthy
of its moment upon the altar, he shouldn't also have his day
in the sun at court.

木瓜心

宛陵有靈根　圓紅珍可玩

衛人感齊恩　瓊琚未容報

15. Quince Heart

Wanling has a spirit root
a round and red and jewel-like fruit
when the state of Wei thanked Ch'i
crimson jade was not repayment

The quince (*Pseudocydonia sinensis*) is a sour applelike fruit that ranges from red to yellow in color. A poem in the *Book of Songs* titled "Quince Heart" was written nearly 3,000 years ago to thank Duke Huan of the state of Ch'i for coming to the aid of the state of Wei. It begins: "You gave us a quince / we return crimson jade / not to repay you / but to deepen our friendship." The "spirit root" (*ling-ken*) refers to the tongue as well as to the ancestor of a state, but I have yet to discover why Sung Po-jen finds it in Wanling or what Wanling has to do with the quince. Wanling was the ancient capital of what is now Anhui province. Perhaps he has Mei Yao-ch'en (1002–1060) in mind — and, of course, his heart. Mei was called "The Gentleman of Wanling" and was responsible, along with Ou-yang Hsiu (1007–1072), for initiating a period of realism in Chinese literature. His poetry, like this book, was often critical of the goings-on at court and advocated reform based on Confucian ideals.

孩兒面

繞脫錦衣褐　童顏嬌可詫

只恐粧鬼時　愛之還又怕

16. Babyface

when their brocade wraps come off
children look so cute
when they act like ghosts
we laugh and then we cringe

Chinese mothers often carry their babies on their backs,
wrapped in blankets with straps they then tie across their
chests. An embroidered blanket suggests the child of a
well-to-do family. Here, the "brocade wrap" also refers to the
perianth, or outer covering, of the plum blossom, which has
just fallen off to reveal the petals before they have begun to
unfold. This poem seems aimed at the young emperor,
Li-tsung (1205–1264), who would have been just over thirty
when this poem was written and whose impulsive, self-
indulgent behavior often raised eyebrows at court.

李

垂垂生井上　遊子休整冠

道旁徒自苦　青眼誰能看

17. Plum

where it hangs above a well
travelers dare not touch their hats
beside a road it languishes
who looks at it with pleasure

The second line paraphrases Ts'ao Chih's "Ballad of a Gentle-man," which begins: "A gentleman takes precautions / he doesn't stay where suspicion reigns / or tie his shoe in a melon field / or adjust his hat beneath a plum tree." In the first couplet, a traveler drinks from a well and looks at the plums overhead with longing. In the second couplet, how-ever, the plum only serves to remind the traveler of his thirst, as the Chinese plum is especially sour. If a fruit such as the plum needs the right location to be appreciated, the same might be said for our author and his work.

瓜

東陵人已仙　黯淡斜陽暮
可慚名利心　孜孜問葵戍

18. Melon

Old Tungling has joined the immortals
into darkness sunlight fades
the shameless quest for profit and fame
the entreaties of Kuei Garrison

During the Ch'in dynasty, Shao P'ing was enfeoffed as the
marquis of Tungling. When the Han dynasty replaced the
Ch'in in 207 B.C., Shao P'ing's status was reduced to that of a
commoner. Undeterred, he supported himself by growing
melons near his former estate east of the capital of Ch'ang-an.
(*Shihchi:* 23) Ever since then, his name has been synonymous
with indifference to worldly success or failure. The *Tsochuan*
(Chuang: 8) records an event five centuries earlier, when Duke
Hsiang, ruler of the state of Ch'i, ordered his followers to
garrison a place called Kueichiu (Hills of Kuei). It was melon
season, and he told them that he would send replacements
the following melon season. When he failed to do so and also
refused their subsequent requests to return home, his follow-
ers plotted rebellion and eventually assassinated the duke.
Sung may be referring here to the garrisons of loyalist rebels
of Shantung province, whom the Southern Sung sometimes
supported against the Jurchens and sometimes against the
Mongols and other times betrayed. The wording of the last
two lines also echoes Mencius, who compares those earnest
in the pursuit of virtue with those equally earnest in the
pursuit of profit (*Mencius:* 7A.25).

螺貝

生長滄波中 收羅向書室
剗藤無不平 秖恐無椽筆

19. Conch Shell

born beneath the ocean waves
brought by net to a scholar's study
vines of Yen all lie flat
but where is a big enough brush

Chinese intellectuals have long appreciated and enjoyed writing about the unusual. Here, a scholar looks for the biggest brush he can find to praise a seashell from the Indian Ocean with as much hyperbole as he can muster. Among the many kinds of paper used in ancient China, the paper made from rattan vines that grew along Chekiang's Yen River was especially prized and reserved for special occasions.

科斗

清波漾蛙子　古書形似之

可惜書廢久　時人無能知

20. Tadpole

a pollywog in crystal water
ancient writing looked like this
out of use so long alas
people now don't know its meaning

Among the means of writing used by the early Chinese over 3,000 years ago was a bamboo stylus that they dipped in black lacquer. In contrast to the more angular characters carved on metal and bone during the same period, these early written forms consisted of black drops and squiggly lines. They continue to require considerable effort to decipher whenever they come to light. Of course, Sung also wonders what else people of his day no longer understand.

Large Buds
EIGHT BRANCHES

琴甲

大葉八枝

高山流水音

泠泠生指下

無與俗人彈

伯牙恐嘲罵

21. Zither Pick

the sound of high mountains or flowing water
crystal notes from a fingertip
play them not for common people
lest you rouse Po-ya's wrath

The Chinese trace the seven-string zither back 5,000 years
to Emperor Fu Hsi, who is also credited with inventing the
trigrams of the *Book of Changes*. The instrument is tradition-
ally played with bamboo picks attached to the forefinger and
thumb. Yu Po-ya played his zither some 3,000 years ago from
a hill overlooking the confluence of the Han River and the
Yangtze. Whenever he played, his friend Chung Tzu-ch'i
knew what was in his heart. Sometimes it was high moun-
tains. Sometimes it was flowing water. When Tzu-ch'i died,
Po-ya smashed his zither, claiming there was no one else
worth playing for. The relationship between these two men
has come to symbolize the truest of friendships — hence the
remark about not playing such music for "common people."
Po-ya's "High Mountains" and "Flowing Water" are still in
the repertoire of Chinese zither players.

藥杵

蟾宮有兔曰　搗藥千萬年
藥有長生術　世人無計傳

22. Pestle

inside Toad Palace there lives a hare
grinding elixir for millions of years
elixir that confers eternal life
beyond the reach of mortals

"Toad Palace" is another name for the moon, which is the
residence of Heng-o (also known as Ch'ang-o), the wife of
Hou-yi. Long ago, one of the daughters of the Queen Mother
of the West gave Hou-yi a pill that conferred immortality. But
she warned him that dire consequences would result if he
swallowed it before he was physically and spiritually ready.
Hou-yi returned home and hid the pill. One day when he was
gone, his wife discovered the pill and swallowed it. It made
her so light, she floated up to the moon, where she turned
into a toad and coughed up the pill, which turned into a hare.
And the hare has been busy ever since grinding more elixir
for Heng-o. Many Chinese emperors spent fortunes in their
quest for such an escape from mortality.

蚌殻

伏與蜎相持　自有山川隔

祝君無孕珠　恐非保身策

23. Oyster Shell

don't quarrel with a snipe
land and water are separate worlds
neither should you give birth to pearls
they won't guard your life

The state of Chao once attacked the state of Yen. The king of Yen proposed launching a counterattack, but his adviser objected and related the following story: An oyster was sunning itself on a riverbank when suddenly a snipe flew down and speared it. But before the snipe could eat the oyster, the oyster slammed shut on the snipe's beak. Neither creature would let go of the other. Eventually, a fisherman came along and made dinner of them both. The adviser said that attacking Chao would only expose Yen to the attack of a third state, which is, in fact, what happened when both Yen and Chao were swallowed by the state of Ch'in in the third century B.C. The Northern Sung, which controlled the arid north, was the realm of land, and the Southern Sung, encompassing the entire watershed of the Yangtze, was the realm of water. It is still known for its production of freshwater pearls.

鶤甫

曳頸吟松梢　何異揚州鶴
胡爲鶴未成　苦被玄裳錯

24. Stork Beak

atop a pine it strains to sing
no different from a Yangchou crane
though a crane it never will be
despite the confusion of its black attire

The crane is a symbol of transcendence, and on its back Taoists fly to the Islands of the Immortals — if, indeed, they do not become cranes themselves. Once at a dinner party, a host asked three guests to reveal their fantasies. One said he imagined himself becoming governor of Yangchou. Another said he imagined himself becoming a fabulously wealthy merchant. The third guest said he imagined himself flying off on a crane. The first guest then revised his fantasy and envisioned himself wrapping strings of coins around his waist and traveling to Yangchou on the back of a crane. Ever since then, the Yangchou crane has been a symbol of greed rather than transcendence. The Chinese stork is similar in appearance to the crane. Both have black plumage on the lower half of their wings and tails. But unlike the crane, the stork can't sing. In fact, it's mute. Thus, the black silk at the bottom of the robes worn by officials, who are themselves mute, reminds Sung of the stork and not the crane.

卣

中尊嚴祀典　幽未裸而實　將裸而實鬱鬯　禮文知有秩

25. Yu

a large bronze dignifies the sacrifice
it's filled before the ch'ang is served
the yi are then filled from this
rituals have their order

In ancient times, the shaman and other participants at a
sacrifice were served an alcoholic beverage called *ch'ang,*
which was distilled from black millet and infused with
turmeric. This beverage was first poured into a large bronze
vessel called a *yu,* which was carried into the ceremony by
means of a bronze handle attached to either side of the vessel
that allowed it to swivel and thus avoid spillage. The ch'ang
was then ladled into smaller bronze vessels called *yi,* from
which the participants drank. In this and the following three
poems Sung reminds his fellow intellectuals of the impor-
tance of the knowledge and observance of ritual usages.

柷

方深有制度 撞之以合樂
止樂憂以致 始終知所覺

26. Chu

sides and depth of fixed dimensions
struck it sets the tune
to stop the music tap the yu
start and finish have their cues

The *chu* and *yu* were among the percussion instruments of
the early Chinese but are now rarely used, except on such
ritual occasions as Confucius' birthday (September 28). The
chu was a square wooden box twenty-nine inches on a side,
twenty-one inches deep, and open at the top. It was struck on
the inside at the beginning of a performance to establish the
beat for the ensemble. The yu was a hollow wooden instru-
ment carved into the shape of a tiger. Its back was tapped to
announce the end of a performance. The yu survives in
Chinese Buddhist ceremonies, where it is used to maintain
the beat. It is no longer shaped like a tiger, but it is still called
a yu, or *mu-yu*. However, the character for *yu* has since been
replaced by a homophone, meaning "fish."

邊

蕃竹緯琅玕

遇祭何所容

為形有如豆

乾桃與脩糗

27. Pien

green bamboo with weft of white
shaped similar to a tou
what does it hold at the sacrifice
dried peaches, meat, and grain

The *pien* consisted of a pedestal woven of rattan or bamboo
and an upper bowl designed to hold four pints of offerings.
Offerings that included sauces were placed inside a similar
vessel, first made of pottery and later of bronze, called a *tou*.
Clay tou dating back 6,000 years have been found among the
earliest Neolithic remains in China. Because of their associa-
tion with longevity, peaches are a favorite offering to the
gods, ancestors, and elders.

爵

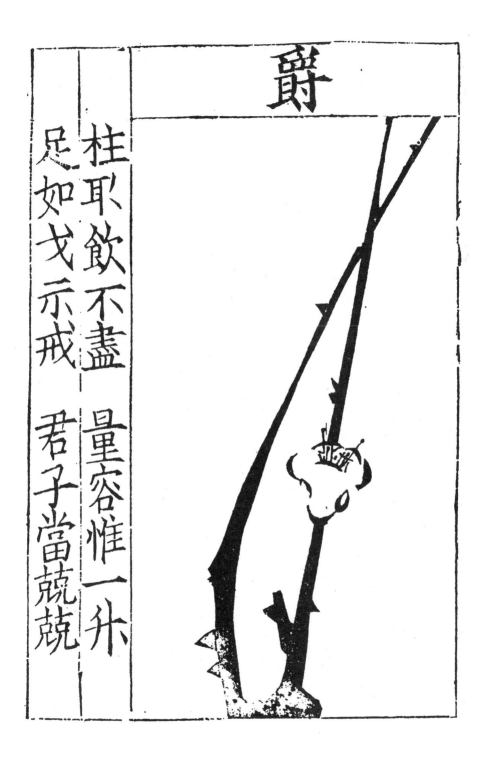

柱耳飲不盡　量容惟一升

足如戈示戒　君子當兢兢

28. Chueh

posts make sure it isn't drained
it only holds a pint
knifelike legs give warning
a gentleman takes care

The *chueh* was a small bronze vessel supported by three bladed feet. It was used to hold the ch'ang mentioned in poem 25 and was originally called an yi. It was renamed by Sung dynasty scholars because it reminded them of a *ch'ueh* (sparrow) whose call sounded like someone saying "stop-stop, enough-enough." They also thought the two posts that protruded from the top of the chueh were meant to come into contact with the drinker's forehead to remind them not to drain the vessel and that overindulgence leads to early death. This may have been true for certain chueh, but most of the vessels unearthed so far have only rudimentary posts. And the earliest ones, dating back 4,000 years, have no posts at all.

Opening

EIGHT BRANCHES

春甕浮香

欲開八枝

斗醉石亦醉　無量不及亂

獨醒誰得知　憔悴滄江畔

29. Jug of Spring Perfume

drunk on a quart drunk on a gallon
the only restriction is avoiding disorder
who would know if you alone are sober
sitting by the river distraught and forlorn

Spring wine is made during the winter from rice or other
grain harvested in autumn. The hill tribes of southwest China
still carry on this tradition, as I can personally attest, which
supplies the means to drive away the winter and to welcome
the spring. Since the alcoholic content of rice wine is rarely
more than 10 percent, someone who gets drunk on a quart is
considered to have a low tolerance. The second line is from
the *Analects* of Confucius, and is about Confucius himself:
"It was only regarding wine that he set no limit, as long as he
wasn't disorderly" (10.8). However, elsewhere in the *Analects*,
Confucius advises his disciples not to be overcome by wine
during a sacrifice (9.15). The last two lines are culled from the
beginning of "The Fisherman," a poem attributed to the poet
Ch'u Yuan (d. 268 B.C.), whose too-frank advice to his ruler
resulted in his exile: "When Ch'u Yuan was banished / he
wandered along rivers / he sang on their banks / distraught
and forlorn / till a fisherman asked / aren't you the Lord of
the Gorges / what fate has brought you to this / and Ch'u
Yuan answered / the world is muddy / I alone am clean /
everyone is drunk / I alone am sober / and so they sent me
away." While Ch'u Yuan is held up as an exemplar of patrio-
tism, Sung chides him here for his self-righteousness, as does
the fisherman, who continues, "if everyone is drunk / drink
up the dregs / why be banished / for deep thought and
purpose."

寒缸吐焰

燈火迫新涼　志士功名重
十年窗下愁　會見金蓮寵

30. Flame from a Winter Brazier

lamplight chases autumn chill
single-minded men see glory
ten hard years beneath a window
favored by a golden lotus

In winter, the Chinese still use charcoal-filled braziers, usually
suspended by wires, to warm themselves in different rooms
of their homes. The title suggests an old scholar still trying
to pass the exams that lead to official appointment. The first
line, from a poem by the Sung dynasty poet Chu Sung, intro-
duces us to a candidate of modest means studying at night in
the light from a neighbor's window and dreaming of arriving
as Ling-hu T'ao once did at the Hanlin Academy, where senior
officials lived. After passing the exams, Ling-hu rose to the
post of chief minister under the T'ang dynasty Emperor
Hsiuan-tsung (r. 846–859), and he served in that capacity for
ten years. One night after Ling-hu had been working late in
the palace, the emperor bestowed on him the singular honor
of being carried back to the Hanlin Academy in the imperial
carriage, which was lit in front by gilded candles shaped like
lotuses. Ling-hu's fellow officials were most impressed.

蝸角

蠻觸國誰雄　戰爭猶未息

由此奪虛名　費盡人間力

31. Snail Horns

which is stronger Man or Ch'u
locked in endless warfare
fighting over empty names
squandering their people's strength

Chuang-tzu once used the example of a snail to urge rulers to avoid war. The horns of a snail, he said, were actually two countries named Man and Ch'u that were engaged in an endless cycle of warfare over control of the empty space that stretched between them (*Chuangtzu: 25*). Another comment on the conflict between the Northern Sung and the Southern Sung.

馬耳

騏驎無伯樂　尖輕徒竹披
北臺深雪裏　且讀坡仙詩

32. Horse Ears

what's Ch'i-chi without Po Le
thin pointed useless knives
on North Terrace half-buried in snow
read the poem of old Tung-p'o

Po Le lived around 900 B.C. and was a famous judge of horses. In his treatise on the subject, he listed the characteristics of a horse's ears as especially indicative of its ability. Their size and sharpness, he said, revealed a horse's stamina and speed. Among the horses whose ears justified his judgment was one named Ch'i-chi, whose name is still synonymous with speed. Scholars seeking official positions have often expressed the hope of finding a ruler as perceptive as Po Le. While visiting the area west of the modern port of Chingtao, Su Tung-p'o once wrote two poems on the wall of Chucheng's North Terrace after a heavy snowfall. In one of them, he wrote that the only things visible above the snow were the twin peaks of nearby Horse Ear Mountain. Sung wonders if his own emperor is as good a judge of men as Po Le was of horses.

篮

祭器古不輕　斯焉盛黍稷
內方而外圓　無乃器之特

33. Kuei

the ancients prized ritual vessels
this one held the millet
inside square and outside round
indeed a unique container

The *kuei* was a wooden vessel used for holding millet during sacrifices. It stood one foot high and had a capacity of one peck and two pints. Its counterpart for holding rice was the *fu*, which had the same capacity but was square on the outside and round on the inside. Rice was the chief grain of the south, while millet was the chief grain of the north. Both vessels were fitted with a lid, on top of which sat a turtle. The turtle symbolized the universe, while in the case of the kuei, the square interior symbolized earth, and the round lid symbolized heaven. Again, Sung begins a series based on the shapes of ceremonial items.

瓚

如盤而柄圭　崇祼以為器

矩鬯次第陳　豈容忘古意

34. Tsan

imagine a bowl with a handle of jade
a ladle for pouring libations
serving the ch'ang one cup at a time
who could forget its ancient meaning

The *tsan* was used during ancestral sacrifices to serve the ch'ang, as explained in poem 25. This particular ritual utensil consisted of a jade handle attached to a bronze bowl ten inches in diameter and with a capacity of five pints. The character *tsan* is made up of two parts: one meaning "jade" and the other meaning "king." According to Taoist mythology, the Jade Emperor is the ruler of Heaven as well as everything below.

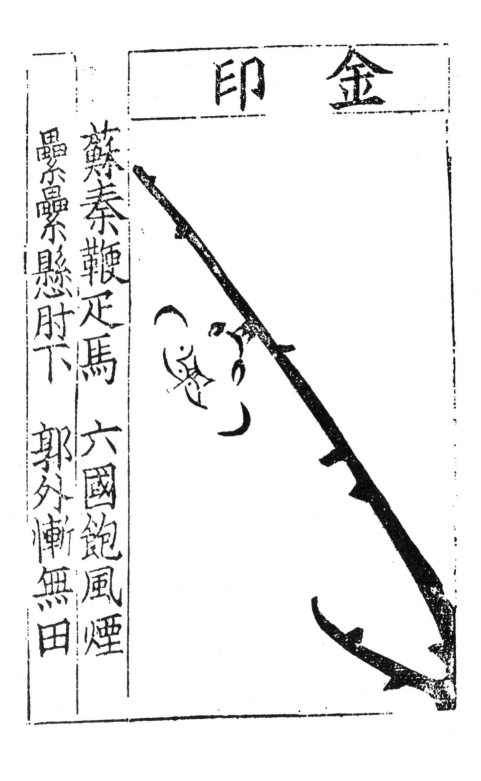

金印

驚秦鞭定馬　六國飽風煙

纍纍纍懸肘下　郭外慚無田

35. Gold Chop

Su Ch'in whipped his horse harder
he raised the dust in six states
authority dangled below his elbow
alas no country retreat

Signatures still have no legal status in China. Only when a
vermilion seal has been affixed with a chop made of metal,
stone, or wood is a document recognized as genuine. In
ancient times, an official's chop was attached to his waist sash
to prevent its misuse. Only a chief minister or his representa-
tive was allowed to use a gold chop. Su Ch'in, who lived in
the fourth century B.C., was an architect of the coalition of
six states that opposed the encroachment of the state of Ch'in,
which eventually swallowed all six and unified all of China
for the first time in 221 B.C. The great authority that Su
wielded, however, depended on his constant travel among the
different states, and he was rarely able to visit his own home
in Loyang. He was murdered while living as a guest in the
state of Ch'i, unlike his teacher, the Taoist Kuei Ku, who
slipped quietly away and lived out his days in anonymity.
To spend one's final years in the countryside was the dream
of most officials in ancient China — and still is today.

玉斗

鴻門罷樽酒　舞劍事還差

范增徒怒撞　漢業成劉家

36. Jade Dipper

at Hungmen the drinking stopped
the sword dance missed its mark
Fan Tseng's fit of rage was useless
the throne of Han belonged to Liu

Hungmen is the name of an opening in the loess plateau east
of the ancient capital of Ch'ang-an. This is where Hsiang Yu
and Liu Pang met in 206 B.C. to divide the empire after
bringing the Ch'in dynasty to an end. At their meeting,
Hsiang Yu planned to assassinate his rival during a sword
dance, but Liu Pang's adviser learned of the plot and con-
vinced Liu to act the fool. Hsiang Yu forgot to give the signal,
and Liu escaped during a visit to the latrine. Before he left,
Liu asked his adviser to present two jade dippers to Fan
Tseng, Hsiang Yu's chief adviser, who had hatched the
assassination plot. Realizing their chance to stop Liu had
slipped away, Fan Tseng smashed the dippers in anger. Not
long afterward, Liu Pang defeated Hsiang Yu and established
the Han dynasty.

Fully Opened

FOURTEEN BRANCHES

舜

大開一十四枚

五采會章服　汝明以垂教

虎蜼宗廟器　于以象其孝

37. Yi

colored silk on formal robes
indicates instruction follows
tigers and monkeys on temple bronzes
symbolize filial piety

The word *yi* was the general term for any bronze vessel used as a cup or a vase during sacrifices in the ancestral temple. Such vessels, cast with monkey or tiger designs, have been traced back some 4,000 years to the time of Emperor Shun. The tigers and monkeys were intended to remind people that even the most vicious and unruly of animals honored their parents. Shun was chosen to succeed Emperor Yao because of his filial piety. With regard to court attire, he is also credited with adding silk robes embroidered with twelve symbols, among them the monkey and the tiger.

黼

象明十二章　斧形不可玩　戴以取其辨　斯以取其斷

38. Fu

symbols take twelve forms
the ax shape isn't mere decoration
double-edged it means distinguish
here it means decide

As mentioned in the previous note, silk robes worn at court were embroidered with twelve symbols that were already ancient when Emperor Shun began using them more than 4,000 years ago. Two symbols are the tiger and the monkey, and another two are axes. The double-edged ax symbolized the ability to distinguish right from wrong, while this single-edged ax, called *fu,* symbolized the power to decide. This is no doubt a comment on imperial vacillation.

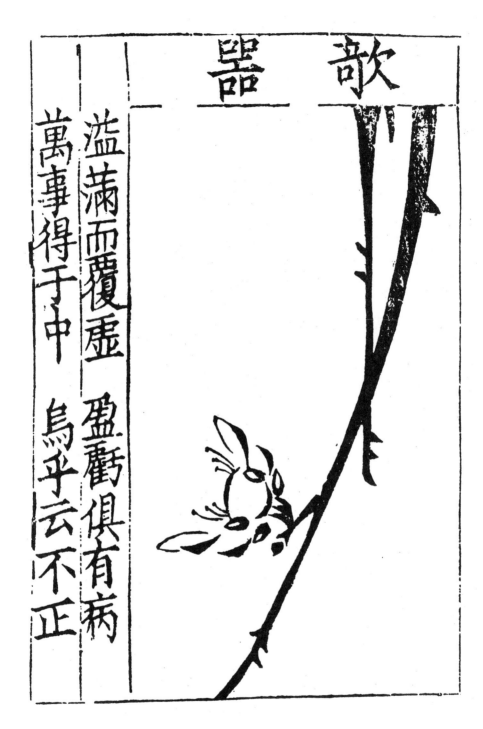

欹器歌

溢滿而覆虛
盈欹俱有病
萬事得于中
烏乎云不正

39. Tilting Bowl

fill it and it empties
deficiency and excess both are ills
all things have their balance
don't think this one isn't right

This "bowl-on-a-swivel" was placed next to the throne to remind the emperor that excess leads to want. Only when the bowl was half-full was it stable. According to Hsun-tzu, Confucius saw a device like this in the ancestral hall of Duke Huan: "An attendant poured water into a container that hung at an angle. As the water level approached the midpoint, the container became upright. But when the attendant went beyond the midpoint, it tipped over, the water poured out, and only after it was empty did it resume its former position. Seeing this, Confucius sighed, 'Alas! Whatever becomes full becomes empty!'" (*Hsuntzu*).

懸鍾

五更山外鳴　斗低殘月小
喚起利名人　僕僕渾無了

40. Hanging Bell

as the Dipper sinks and the crescent fades
from the hills it sings at dawn
calling to those seeking profit and fame
the treadmill never ends

This type of bell can be found in Buddhist temples, where it still announces services before dawn. It was struck by swinging a log against its exterior rather than by pulling a clapper against its interior. Although every city had its quota of temples, most were built beyond city walls and the world of red dust so that their residents might have an easier time freeing themselves of delusion, desire, and anger, the poisons that perpetuate rebirth on the Wheel of Life and Death. Treadmills were used in China since ancient times to move water to higher elevations.

扇

九華井六角　流傳名不同

無如慰黎庶　爲我揚仁風

41. Fan

Nine Flowers and Six Corners
hand down different names
better would be to soothe the people
to stir for all a gentle breeze

According to Ts'ao Chih (192–232), Emperor Huan (r. 147–
168) of the Han dynasty gave a fan described as having nine
flowers painted on it to his father, Ts'ao Ts'ao (155–220). It was
Ts'ao Ts'ao who brought the Han dynasty to an end. Given the
dates, either Ts'ao Chih misremembered or his father did.
Two centuries later, a man offered to inscribe the six-cornered
fans that an old lady was selling along a promenade. To her
surprise, she then sold the fans for a small fortune. The man
turned out to be Wang Hsi-chih (303–361), China's most
famous calligrapher. Thus the name Nine Flowers is associ-
ated with misfortune and the name Six Corners with good
fortune. Also in the fourth century, the famous writer-official
Yuan Hung, on being presented with a fan to use for the
journey to a new post, said "Rather may it stir a gentle breeze
to soothe the people."

盤

水精行素鱗　琉璃走夜光
銘垂日日新　萬古稽商湯

42. Basin

swimming silver fins in crystal
glassy luminescence
engraved *renew each day*
the ages bow to T'ang of Shang

Bronze basins were used for washing the face and hands
during rituals, and their inner surface was often cast with
turtles, fish, and other aquatic creatures. Inscribed on Emperor
T'ang's washbasin were the words: "May you renew yourself
today, renew yourself day after day, renew yourself every day."
T'ang overthrew the Hsia dynasty in 1750 B.C. and founded
the Shang dynasty, which he named after the small fiefdom
where he began his rebellion. T'ang's quest for self-renewal
continues to inspire the Chinese, as it did Sun Yat-sen, the
first president of the Republic of China, who took the name
Jih-hsin ("Renew Each Day") during his early years.

向 日

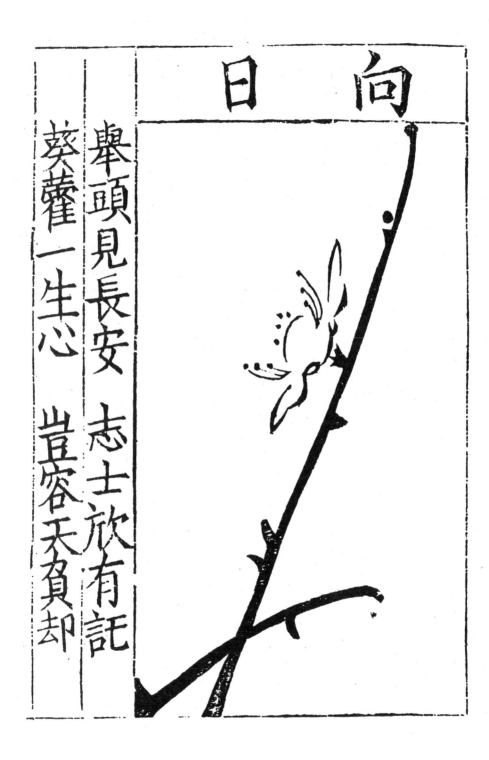

向日

葵 舉頭見長安

蘤 志士欣有託

一 生 心

豈 容 天 貞 却

43. Facing the Sun

lifting their eyes toward Ch'ang-an
truehearted men await a mission
peas and sunflowers have one thought
how can Heaven turn away

Located beneath the streets of modern Sian, Ch'ang-an was the capital of eleven dynasties and the center of the Chinese universe from the time it was first established in 200 B.C. until it was destroyed in A.D. 907. During that time, it was the biggest city in the ancient world, with two million residents. More than three centuries later, Sung Po-jen and his fellow expatriates south of the Yangtze dreamed of driving the barbarians from north China and reuniting the country, with Ch'ang-an as its capital. Peas and sunflowers are heliotropic, and members of China's official class often referred to themselves as such, always looking toward the Son of Heaven. Here, Sung bemoans the royal reluctance to take up the challenge of reunification.

擎露

僊掌在何處　徒成千載羞
唯有故園菊　沾濡當九秋

44. Collecting Dew

what happened to the Immortal's Palm
a thousand years of useless shame
the ancient garden is filled with mums
drenched with dew on Double Ninth

The drinking of dew, the purer the better, was considered
efficacious in prolonging life. To this end, in the second
century B.C., Emperor Wu constructed a tower of cedar
beams and bronze pillars more than 200 feet high. And on
top of this tower, he placed a bronze basin to collect the dew
of the gods. The basin became known as the Immortal's Palm
and was most likely buried with Emperor Wu at Maoling,
some 25 miles west of Sian. This wasn't the only extravagance
indulged in by Emperor Wu during his search for immortal-
ity, and Sung voices the Confucian disdain for the waste of
public funds on such personal fantasies. The Chinese words
for "chrysanthemum," "old," and "nine" were all once homo-
phones and in some dialects still are. On the ninth day of the
ninth month (nine being the ultimate yang, or male, number,
and the combination of two nines being especially auspicious),
Chinese men still celebrate their longevity with spirits
infused with chrysanthemums.

鼎

郟鄏至汾陰
天下望調羹
重名垂不朽
有誰能着手

45. Tripod

from Chiaju to Fenyin
their fame comes down intact
the world hungers for a chef
someone who can cook

With its three legs supporting a round or square body, the
tripod first appeared in Neolithic times as a clay cooking pot
that was heated from underneath. In addition to its use in
preparing the family meal, it was also used for presenting
offerings to ancestors. As the second function began to take
precedence over the first, tripods were made of bronze at
great expense, and the possession of such a vessel conferred
the right to conduct sacrifices to clan ancestors. Around 1000
B.C., King Ch'eng of the Chou dynasty set up a tripod just
west of Loyang at Chiaju to establish his clan's authority over
the Yellow and Huai River floodplains. Fenyin is the name of
a place in Shansi province where, in the second century B.C.,
a tripod was unearthed that reportedly belonged to the
Yellow Emperor, who reigned around 2600 B.C. and who
established the hegemony of the Han Chinese in China.
Confucius and his followers considered the period between
the Yellow Emperor's reign and the beginning of the Chou
dynasty as China's age of sage rulers, who were often likened
to chefs in that they blended competing interests into one
harmonious whole. And plums were often used in cooking,
as noted in the *Book of Documents,* which says, "Be my salt
and plums in seasoning the soup" (4.8).

鏞

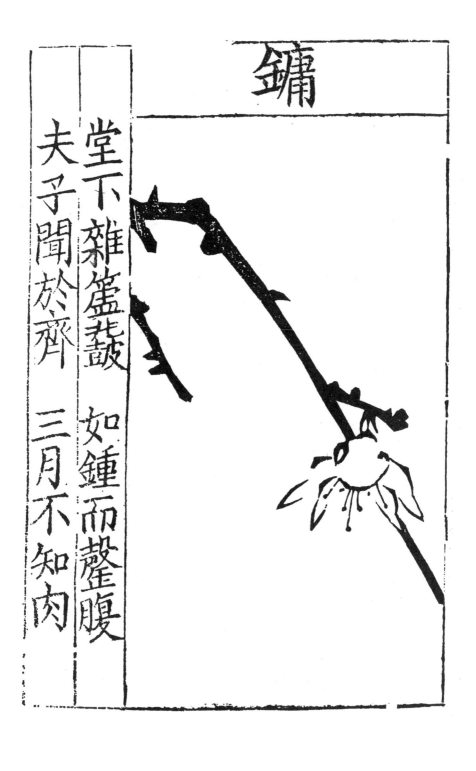

堂下雜簨鼓　如鍾而聲腹

夫子聞於齊　三月不知肉

46. Yung

among the palace rattle drums
hangs this empty-bellied bell
Confucius heard it once in Ch'i
for ninety days he ate no meat

In 517 B.C. Confucius left his own state of Lu during a period
of political instability and took up residence in Lintzu, the
capital of the neighboring state of Ch'i. While he was there,
he heard a style of music first developed by the music master
of Emperor Shun 1,700 years earlier. The music was called
Shao, and Confucius was so overwhelmed by its sound that
he didn't pay attention to food for three months. Although
primarily orchestrated for wind instruments, it included
drums (especially handheld rattle drums struck by balls
suspended on either side of the barrel) and bells. This particu-
lar bell, known as a *yung,* doesn't have a clapper inside but is
suspended from a wooden frame and struck from the outside.
It was used at court and in Confucian temples.

麋角

麋鹿同呴呴　山林風雨秋

虋鹿同呴呴　山林風雨秋

姑蘇臺上月　子胥曾約遊

47. Antlers

the stags and does all bleat
the woods and mist say fall
the moon above Kusu Tower
where Wu Tzu-hsu once strolled

Deer normally breed in the fall. Kusu, or Lingyenshan, as it is now called, is the name of a hill nine miles southwest of Suchou in Kiangsu province. During the fifth century B.C., King Fu Ch'ai of the state of Wu turned the hill into a deer park. After defeating the state of Yueh to the south, he built a palace and a huge tower on the hill and spent much of his time banqueting there with his new concubine, Hsi Shih, a gift of the king of Yueh. His chief minister, Wu Tzu-hsu, criticized him for his dalliance and later paid for his frank advice with his life. While Fu Ch'ai is vilified for his failure to heed such advice, Wu Tzu-hsu is much revered by the people of Suchou, as it was he who chose Suchou as the site for the capital of Wu.

臂猿

一聲長嘯罷　霜月凄林屝
與鶴每相問　貴人胡未歸

48. Gibbon Arm

where their howls still echo
and gates are few below a winter moon
she asks each crane she meets
why hasn't my lord returned

According to the Taoist text *Paoputzu,* a Chinese army
entered the mountains of southern China around 1000 B.C.
and was never seen again. The officers, it was said, turned
into gibbons and cranes, and the soldiers became insects and
sand. Sung is probably referring to the armies sent off to fight
the Jurchens and the Mongols that likewise never returned.
Gibbons were once common in the mountains of the south-
ern half of China, and travelers reported hearing their eerie
howls the entire length of the Yangtze Gorges until modern
times. Cranes also refer to Taoist recluses, whose huts can
still be found among China's hills and mountains.

蘡眉

西施無限愁　後人何必傚
只好笑呵呵　不搵紅粧貌

49. Pinched Eyebrows

why must others imitate
Hsi Shih's constant frown
better just to giggle
it won't ruin your rouge

Hsi Shih was one of the most famous beauties of ancient
China. In the fifth century B.C., the king of Yueh presented
her to his nemesis, the king of Wu, hoping she would distract
him from attending to government affairs, which she did,
much to the king of Wu's regret. Among her famous attri-
butes were pinched eyebrows, reportedly caused by a heart
condition. When other women heard how beautiful she was,
they tried to copy her frown but only succeeded in making
themselves look foolish.

側百

相見是非多　但傍
庶無人共知　鼻
梅花喜神譜卷上終

50. Profile

face-to-face is problematic
from the side the view is clearer
otherwise neither would know
the length of the other's nostrils

An old Chinese adage advises, "From the side the view is clear / from in front no one sees." The Chinese practice of physiognomy assigns great importance to the length of a person's nostrils, with longer nostrils indicating greater depth of character.

Radiant

TWENTY-EIGHT BRANCHES

開鏡

梅花喜神譜卷下　雪岩
爛熳二十八枝

塵匣啓菱花
醜妍無不識
羞殺幾英雄
霜鬒太煎逼

51. Open Mirror

lifting the ling flower from its case
revealing the lovely and ugly
frightening how many heroes
with the sudden attack of white hair

Bronze mirrors entered China via the Silk Road as early as 4,000 years ago and remained the primary means of reflection until the eighteenth century, when they were finally replaced by those of glass. These early bronze mirrors were rarely bigger than a person's hand but were sufficiently convex to reflect the whole face. The back was covered with symbols and designs and included a protruding boss in the middle with a cord through it that allowed the mirror to be picked up from its protective box without getting fingerprints on the polished side. Most mirrors were round, but a popular shape during the T'ang and Sung dynasties was the eight-petaled ling flower, or water caltrop (*Trapa bicornis*). It reminded those who used it of the purity of water and of water's ability to reflect their true appearance.

覆杯

誰嘆月娟娟
霜天閒却手

醉者未能醒
不必重斟酒

52. Overturned Cup

who sighs "the moon is lovely"
as it slips through the winter sky
a drunk incapable of being sober
no need to pour him more wine

Sung Po-jen must have had someone in mind when he wrote
this poem. Perhaps it was Li Pai, the poet of wine, who
drowned, so one story goes, trying to embrace the moon in
the waters of the Yangtze.

晃

充鷺毛希玄

璪取玉以文

君尊十二旒

五采宗成周

53. Mien

the yen and the pi, the ts'ui, hsi and hsuan
twelve strands distinguish a king's
adorned with pendants of jade
five colors to honor Chengchou

The *mien* was a flat-topped hat worn by emperors and high-ranking officials. The first line lists five types. The *yen* was worn at sacrifices to former kings, the *pi* at sacrifices to one's father, the *ts'ui* at sacrifices to the rivers and mountains of the four directions, the *hsi* at sacrifices to the gods of the soil and grain and to the five household spirits, and the *hsuan* at all minor sacrifices. Jade beads hung along the front edge of these hats on five, seven, nine, or twelve colored silk strands. The number depended on the wearer's status, with twelve reserved for kings and emperors. The use of five colors (black, white, red, blue, and yellow) goes back to the Chou dynasty, whose eastern capital was at Chengchou near the modern city of Loyang. Once when someone asked Confucius how a state should be governed, he replied, "Implement the calendar of the Hsia dynasty, use the axle width of the Shang dynasty, and wear the flat-topped hat [mien] of the Chou dynasty" (*Analects:* 15.10).

胄

秀鐵壓肩寒　中原思未報

何日掃邊塵　別墨朝天帽

54. Helmet

mail lies cold upon our shoulders
reminding us the plains aren't ours
when will we sweep border dust
another helmet turns toward Heaven

The helmet consisted of a peaked cap with flaps that hung down the sides and the back of the neck. The cap was usually made of metal, and the flaps were made of beaten leather or finely linked mail. When this book was written, the Mongols had just wrested the vast Yellow River and Huai River floodplains from the Jurchens. A century earlier, the Jurchens had seized them from the Chinese, who then retreated south of the Yangtze to Hangchou. The Son of Heaven's inability or unwillingness to retake the plains and drive the barbarians back beyond the old borders was a source of great disappointment to his followers. Their hopes would finally be crushed by the Mongols, who defeated the Jurchens in 1234 and completed their conquest of China in 1276.

並桃

漢帝欲成仙　王毋從天下

結實動千年　三偷尤可詫

55. Pair of Peaches

the Emperor of Han wished to become immortal
the Queen Mother came down from Heaven
bringing fruits that took a thousand years to ripen
imagine stealing three

The Queen Mother of the West, Hsi-wang-mu, was the chief divinity of the Kunlun Mountains in Central Asia. In addition to various magic powers, she possessed the elixir of immortality, which she dispensed in the form of peaches that took up to 3,000 years to ripen. Although she has been variously identified with Arabia's Queen of Sheba and the Greek goddess Hera, the Chinese describe her as having the tail of a panther and the teeth of a tiger. During the Chou dynasty, King Mu visited her at her palace in northern Afghanistan, and she returned the favor 800 years later, when she visited Emperor Wu of the Han dynasty and brought with her seven peaches. She presented four to the emperor and kept three for herself. No Chinese emperor spent more time or wealth trying to attain immortality, and numerous stories about Emperor Wu's quest appeared in subsequent centuries. In one such story, his adviser, Tung-fang Shuo, steals three of the Queen Mother's peaches, but they fall out of his robe as he prepares to leave her palace. In another version, a dwarf presented at court brags to Tung-fang that he also stole three of the Queen Mother's immortal fruits.

雙荔

繪殼爛緗枝

玉真望甘鮮

夏菓收新綠

不管郵兵哭

56. Pair of Lychees

embroidered shells on golden branches
summer fruit with new green leaves
Yu-chen wanted something luscious
she didn't care if couriers suffered

The semitransparent, white fruit of the lychee is enclosed by
a thin red shell. A semitropical fruit, it grows only in China's
southernmost provinces. Yang Yu-chen, known to history as
Yang Kui-fei, was Emperor Hsuan-tsung's favorite concubine.
Among her indulgences were lychees, and it took several
hundred relay riders to keep her supplied during the summer,
when the fruit was in season. When the An Lu-shan Rebellion
broke out in A.D. 755, Yu-chen was blamed for Hsuan-tsung's
extravagant use of public funds and his inattention to govern-
ment. She was strangled during the emperor's flight from the
capital and buried at the side of the road. Her grave is forty
miles west of Sian and still attracts occasional visitors. Sung
may also be referring here to his own emperor's infatuation
with Lady Chia (aka Chia Kui-fei) and his inattention to
government affairs.

鳳朝天

覽輝千仞高　君子思在治
朝陽如不鳴　敢言當自愧

57. Phoenix Facing Heaven

beholding light in the firmament
a gentleman thinks of order
if at dawn he fails to sing
let the shame be his

The phoenix only appears when a virtuous ruler sits on the throne and order prevails in the world. The Son of Heaven traditionally conducted the business of court before dawn. All senior officials in the capital were expected to attend, and those with complaints or recommendations were encouraged to present them at that time. Lines by the Han dynasty poet Chia Yi — "the phoenix soars high in the sky / beholding the light of virtue it descends" — which lament the death of Ch'u Yuan, who was exiled for his unwelcome advice, seem to have inspired Sung's opening line.

蛛掛網

經緯出天機　畫簷斜掛算

可惜巧於蠹　無補人間世

58. Spider on a Web

its weavings inspired by Heaven
hang in the shade of painted eaves
more clever than a silkworm
alas no help to humanity

In ancient China, sumptuary regulations restricted the use of painted designs under the eaves of dwellings to the nobility. The Chinese date the invention of silk to the time of the Yellow Emperor, who reigned around 2600 B.C. One day his wife, Lei-tsu, was drinking tea when a silkworm cocoon fell from a mulberry branch into her cup. While trying to remove it, she began unreeling the cocoon and discovered the secret of making silk thread. The traditional attribution notwithstanding, silkworms appear in China's archaeological record at least 2,000 years before Lei-tsu's time. The spider, meanwhile, meets Chuang-tzu's qualification for attaining old age by being useless to humankind (*Chuangtzu*: 4). Here, however, Sung sees something more nefarious in the spider's clandestine work.

漁笠

艤艇白鷗邊　寒雨敲青篛

駁浪不回頭　方識江湖樂

59. Fisherman's Hat

anchored out among the gulls
cold rain lashing his hat of leaves
he doesn't mind fearsome waves
since discovering the joys afloat

The fisherman's hat is made of bamboo leaves attached to a frame of bamboo strips. Ever since Confucius attributed kindness to the person who loves mountains and wisdom to the one who loves water (*Analects*: 6.21), the love of water has been synonymous with detachment from social convention and with the life of the vagabond or recluse. And nowhere was the water-loving vagabond or recluse more at home than in the lower reaches of the Yangtze, where the Sung court was located.

熊　掌

八珍風味清　蔾腸豈曾識
堪嗤骨爾人　欲與魚兼得

60. Bear Paw

subtlest of the eight rare dishes
it never sees a commoner's stomach
man alas wants his meat
and wants his fish as well

Along with such metaphorical dishes as dragon liver and
phoenix marrow, bear paws were included among the eight
delicacies reserved for special banquets. Mencius said, "I
love fish, and I love bear paws. If I can't have both, I will give
up fish for bear paws. I love life, and I love righteousness.
If I can't have both, I will give up life for righteousness"
(*Mencius:* 6A.10).

飛蟲刺花

花香專引蝶　非蝶亦飛來

顧影不知耻　良為貪者哀

61. Flying Insect Stings a Flower

a flower's scent brings butterflies
something else arrives as well
vanity that knows no shame
and grief born of desire

The flower in this case represents narcissistic love, while the flying insect, in this case a bee, is meant to remind us of sexual predators attracted by the flower's public display of beauty. Desire is one of the greatest dangers to those who strive to cultivate tranquillity. The *Kuoyu* says, "Righteousness is the source of profit. Desire is the origin of regret."

孤鴻叫月

足下一封書　子卿歸自虜
雖曰誰單于　孤忠傳萬古

62. Lone Goose Calling to the Moon

a letter tied to a goose's foot
gained Tzu-ch'ing his freedom
though they say he tricked the khan
the ages call him honest

In 105 B.C. Su Tzu-ch'ing (aka Su Wu) was sent as an envoy to parley with the Hsiung-nu, who occupied parts of northwest China and threatened trade on the Silk Road. But when Su refused to acknowledge the superiority of the nomadic kingdom, the Hsiung-nu khan made him his prisoner. Even when peaceful relations were established twenty years later, the khan continued to deny knowledge of Su Tzu-ch'ing's whereabouts. Finally, Su Tzu-ch'ing managed to get word of his existence to the new Chinese envoy, together with a plan for his release. Su suggested the envoy tell the khan that during a hunt the Chinese emperor shot a wild goose and found a letter from Su Tzu-ch'ing attached to its foot. When the envoy did as Su suggested, the khan had no choice but to order Su's release. Sung is calling on the court either for more trickery in its dealings with the Mongols or for something more than the mere appearance of honesty among its officials.

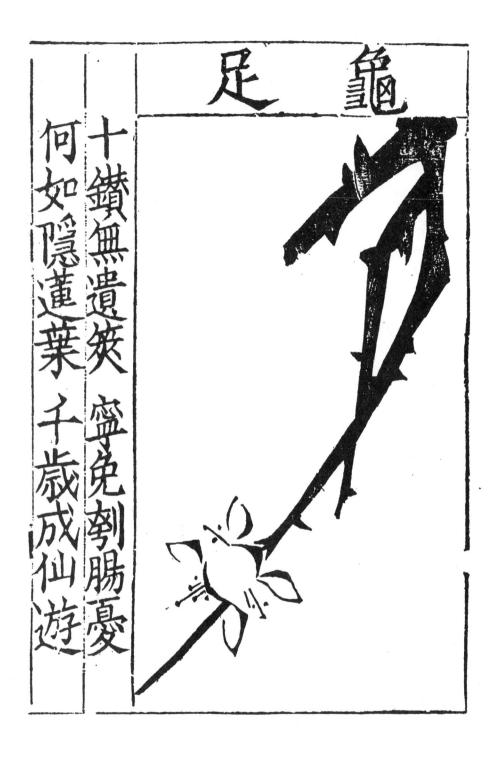

龜足

十鑽無遺筴　窒兔剜腸憂
何如隱蓮葉　千歲成仙遊

63. Turtle Feet

a shell full of holes
or freedom from knives
better to hide beneath lily pads
to wander as an immortal for thousands of years

Turtles were thought to live thousands of years and to possess knowledge of the future. To access this knowledge, the Chinese drilled and heated the turtle's carapace and plastron and interpreted the resulting cracks to predict coming events. Once, when Chuang-tzu was fishing along the Pu River, two emissaries from the state of Ch'u approached him and said, "Our lord wishes to entrust administration of his realm to you." Without bothering to put down his fishing pole, Chuang-tzu replied, "I've heard that your king has a 3,000-year-old turtle shell he keeps on his ancestral altar. Do you think the turtle would rather be dead and have its shell so honored or be alive and dragging its tail in the mud? Leave me be. I would rather drag my tail in the mud" (*Chuangtzu:* 17).

龍爪

著生望雲霓　難作池中物

孔明臥隆中　天子勢亦屈

64. Dragon Claws

a pond can't hold this creature
when the people look for rainbows
but in Lungchung while K'ung-ming slept
even an emperor's might was humbled

Referring to one of China's earliest political heroes, Mencius said, "The people looked to Emperor T'ang as they did to rainbows during a drought" (*Mencius:* 1B.11). Dragons are thought to control the rain and are said to live in deep water. Hence, a pond isn't likely to hold a young dragon for long. Men of great talent are also likened to dragons, and the last two lines are about one such man, Chu-ko Liang (181–234), who was also called K'ung-ming. Chu-ko Liang lived as a hermit near the village of Lungchung in Hupei province. People said he was a sleeping dragon capable of great things, and Liu Pei, the future emperor of the Shu-han dynasty, resolved to see for himself. Twice Liu Pei visited Chu-ko Liang's hut, and twice Chu-ko Liang declined to get up to open the door. Only on the third visit did the two men finally meet. Later, as Liu Pei's chief adviser, Chu-ko Liang left no doubt that he was one of the greatest strategists the world has ever known. On one occasion, he drove off an army of 200,000 with a handful of men and his zither. In this case, Sung suggests it is for the people and not for the emperor that men of ability show themselves.

羽拍雞林

三拍羽翎寒　風雨不改度

起舞何人斯　男兒當自礪

65. Rooster in the Woods Flaps Its Wings

wings flap three times in the frigid air
wind and rain make no difference
who is this getting up to dance
full-grown men don't stay in bed

In a poem in the *Book of Songs* titled "Wind and Rain," a cock crows in the cold three times, each time reminding the listener of a friend and reminding him not to let his affection change. Tsu T'i served as a general in the early years of the fourth century A.D. and never avoided a chance for adventure. When he was younger and serving in the capital of Loyang, he slept under the same blanket with his comrade-in-arms, Liu K'un. Whenever they heard a cock crow, even if it was the middle of the night, they both got up and danced. Sung likewise sees himself getting up early to join other like-minded men but leaves it up to us to imagine what calls them forth. Perhaps it was to attend court. Perhaps it was to serarch for plum blossoms.

松鶴唳天

赤壁夢醒時　兩灑玄裳濕
聲欲聞于天　故向松梢立

66. Crane on a Pine Crying to Heaven

waking from a Red Cliff dream
black robe soaked with rain
trying to reach Heaven's ear
it stands atop a pine

During one of several periods of exile, the eleventh-century poet Su Tung-p'o wrote two poems about his visit to a place on the Yangtze called Red Cliff — not the scene of the famous battle upriver from Wuhan but a place of the same name downriver. In the second of these poems, Su sees a crane fly overhead, and later that night in a dream the crane turns into a black-robed Taoist immortal. The Chinese believe the crane lives hundreds of years and is the transformed embodiment of a person who has attained the Taoist goal of immortality. Although its body is white, the crane's neck and wing tips are black. In a poem in the *Book of Songs* titled "Cry of the Crane," the chance of a person who cultivates the Tao in obscurity coming to the attention of the emperor is likened to a crane's cry being heard in Heaven.

新荷濺雨

新綠小池沼　田田浮翠錢
雨中珠萬顆　巧婦其能穿

67. New Lily Pads in Pouring Rain

a small pond newly green
pads of floating jadelike coins
in the rain ten thousand pearls
only a clever wife could string

"Clever wife" is another name for the tailorbird, which builds
its nest with great skill out of next to nothing. Here, Sung
Po-jen calls on it to fashion a necklace from raindrops.

老菊披霜

世久無淵明　黃花為誰好

青女自凌威　寒香未容老

68. Old Chrysanthemum with Coat of Frost

no Yuan-ming for ages now
for whom do the yellow flowers bloom
once the Blue Girl looms above
their winter perfume won't last long

The chrysanthemum, which blooms in the ninth lunar month, has become a symbol of old age, as its name (according to the ancient pronunciation) was a homophone for the Chinese word for "old." It was the favorite flower of the poet T'ao Yuan-ming (365–427), who immortalized its yellow petals in his poetry and infused them in his wine. The Jade Maiden of the Blue Sky is the spirit that controls the frost and snow. The shorter form of her name, used here, is also another name for the ninth month.

瑟

點異三子　鏗爾舍而作

江上數峰青　湘靈徒寂寞

69. Zither

Tien was different from the others
putting his zither aside he rose
peaks of green along the river
the Spirits of the Hsiang sigh in vain

Tien was the sobriquet of Tseng Hsi, a disciple of Confucius. One day Confucius asked several of his students what they desired most. All replied that they wanted positions of authority, except Tien. When it was his turn, he put down his zither, rose to his feet, and said he would like to go with a group of young men to the countryside in spring, wash away the dust of the past year in the river, dry off in the breeze at the rain-dance altar, and return home singing. Confucius sighed and said he was with Tien (*Analects:* 11.25). The last two lines recall a poem titled "Drum and Zither of the Hsiang River Spirits," by the eighth-century poet Ch'ien Ch'i. His poem includes the refrain, "The song is over the players gone / peaks of green along the river." The song was about Emperor Shun's two wives, who lived some 4,000 years ago and who often entertained their husband with their zithers. When Shun, who was revered as one of China's sage emperors, died, they drowned themselves in the Hsiang River. Ever since then, they have been worshiped as the river's twin spirits. Their grave is on a small island in the middle of Tungting Lake, which is formed by the Hsiang and several other rivers, and which in turn empties into the Yangtze. China's first great poet, Ch'u Yuan, also drowned himself in a nearby tributary of the same river in the third century B.C., and no doubt Sung had his spirit in mind as well. Here, Sung also bemoans the absence of a sage emperor.

鼓

嫠嫠和歌管　責樏無復存

堪笑不知量　以布過雷門

70. Drum

boom-boom goes with voice and flute
mud-filled drumsticks though are lacking
ridiculous so out of place
a drum of cloth at Thunder Gate

In the fifth century B.C., King Kou Chien of the state of Yueh
ordered construction of a huge drum to outdo one in the
neighboring state of Wu, which had earlier defeated Yueh. The
drum, made from the hide of a giant bull, was nine meters in
circumference. Its sound was said to carry all the way to the
Chou dynasty capital of Loyang, a distance of 600 miles.
Before it was destroyed in the fourth century A.D., the drum
was kept in Yueh's ancient capital of Shaohsing at Thunder
Gate. Drumsticks for such large drums were made of woven
bamboo and filled with mud. Not only are such drumsticks
lacking here, the drum itself has been replaced by one made
of cloth. The Han dynasty scholar Wang Tsun once described
a fool as someone who beats a cloth drum at Thunder Gate.
No doubt, Sung has in mind the foolishness of certain would-
be drummers at court.

蜂腰

紫陌暖風細　露旁山更深
蜜甜不知味　萬花空損心

71. Bee's Waist

a fresh breeze warms purple paths
beehives too in distant hills
if their honey isn't tasted
ten thousand flowers give their hearts in vain

The "purple paths" are those of the capital, down which
royalty rode in splendor. The warm breeze of spring suggests
the beginning of a new reign or at least new policies and the
invitation for men of virtue to come out of retirement and
present themselves at court. Reclusion has always been an
option for such men during periods when the court was not a
place of virtue. Hermits in China still make their huts out of
mud, and here the "beehives" refer to their places of solitude
and not, as it might seem, to places of activity. A "bee's waist"
refers to an error of versification where the second and fifth
syllables in a five-syllable line of poetry have the same tone,
which makes it sufficiently difficult to stress the third and
fourth syllables to the point where they almost disappear —
hence, their resemblance to a bee's waist. The last line of the
Chinese exemplifies such an error.

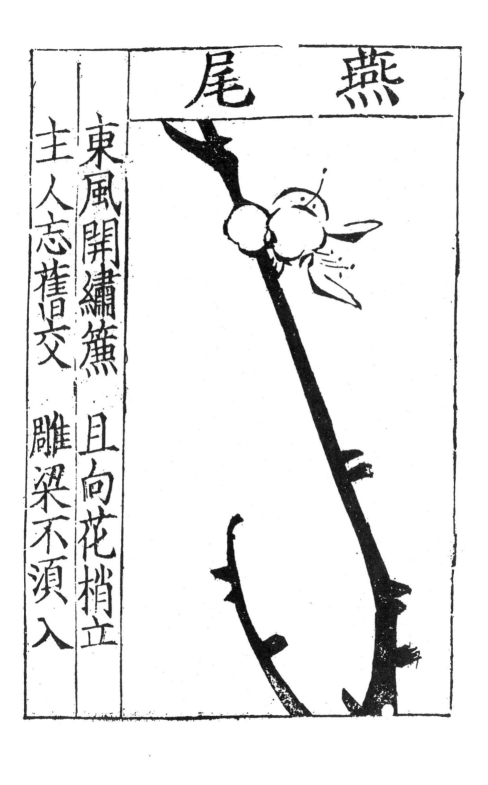

燕尾

東風開繡簾　且向花梢立

主人忘舊交　雕梁不須入

72. Swallowtail

where the east wind parts embroidered curtains
it perches on a flowering branch
where it finds false-hearted friends
it avoids their painted beams

The east wind blows in spring and is the wind of success in
China. This is also when swallows return with their annual
promise of good fortune for the dwellings they choose for
their nests. "Embroidered curtains" and "painted beams"
refer to the dwellings of the rich. The poet Wu Kuan once
wrote: "butterflies fill a branch in bloom / then leave when
flowers fade / only swallows once again / return to dwellings
of the poor."

驚鷗振翼

雪羽卧晴沙　漁人無可慮
機事亦難忘　不如且飛去

73. Frightened Gull Flaps Its Wings

white wings sleep on a sunny shore
the fisherman means no harm
but subterfuge is hard to suppress
best for now to fly away

The Taoist philosopher Lieh-tzu (*circa* fifth century B.C.) tells
this story: "There once was a young man who lived by the sea
and who loved seagulls. Whenever he walked along the shore,
more than a hundred birds would follow him. One day his
father asked him to catch a few and bring them back to keep
as pets. The next day, when the young man went walking
along the shore, not a single gull would approach him"
(*Liehtzu: 2*).

野鶻翻身

很禽忘所傳　翻身擎鳥雀
羽毛同所天　何苦強凌弱

74. Wheeling Hawk

a bird of prey forgets its kind
it wheels and grabs a pigeon
feathered creatures share the sky
why this effort to oppress the weak

The use of hawks and falcons for hunting is still common among nomadic peoples in China but was once the prerogative of the nobility. In addition to serving as emblems of authority, birds of prey also call to mind the rapaciousness of the powerful regarding the less fortunate.

顧步

世道多巇嶇　進趨思退却

一步一回頭　庶無輕失脚

75. Pondering the Next Step

perilous are all worldly paths
advancing think of turning back
with every step a look behind
no more careless stumbles

The path to worldly success is not the path recommended
by Confucius, Lao-tzu, or other Chinese sages. Concerning
the ancient masters of the Tao, Lao-tzu wrote, "I describe
them with reluctance / they were careful as if crossing a
river in winter / cautious, as if worried about neighbors"
(*Taoteching:* 15).

掩　粧

粉黛巧粧施　菱花還自照

底事不爭妍　又恐西施笑

76. Applying Makeup

skilled at applying powder and paint
gazing at themselves in ling-flower mirrors
if no one fought over beauty
Hsi Shih would likely smile

Bronze mirrors in the shape of the eight-petaled water caltrop flower (see poem 51) were popular in the Sung dynasty. Hsi Shih was one of ancient China's most famous beauties. But her charm, it was said, came from her constant frown.

晴空掛月

萬里收纖雲　一鈎懸碧落

缺圓無定時　人間幾愁樂

77. Crescent Moon in a Clear Sky

no trace of clouds for a thousand miles
a hook hangs in an azure sky
waxing and waning without cease
along with how many joys and sorrows

K'ang T'ing-chih's "Ode to the Moon" begins, "Before the terrace a suspended mirror / beyond the curtain a hanging hook."

遙山抹雲

無心出岫時　山腰橫一抹
爲霖覆手間　豈容留旱魃

78. Clouds Sweeping Distant Mountains

aimlessly rolling out of mountain caves
one wave and the slopes are gone
changing to mist with the turn of a hand
how could the demon of drought last long

The first line is from T'ao Yuan-ming's "The Return": "Look-
ing up I gaze into the distance / clouds aimlessly roll out of
mountain caves." The second line quotes Huang Keng's
"Evening Stroll in the West Garden in Spring": "When the
last crimson rays fade / one wave and the mountain is gone."
The third line comes from Tu Fu's "Ballad of Poor Friends":
"A turn of the hand and clouds appear / another turn and
they become rain." And the last line recalls "River of Clouds"
in the *Book of Songs:* "The demon of drought is cruel / like
fire, like flames."

Fading

SIXTEEN BRANCHES

會星介

欲謝一十六枚

星會飾以王　燦燦光朝儀

重臣頭似雪　左右應皐夔

79. Star-Lined Hat

set with stars and adorned with jade
glittering lights of morning court
men of rank with heads of snow
Kao and K'uei on the left and right

This particular hat was made of leather triangles sewn together with jewels along the seams. It was worn by senior officials during their dawn audience with the emperor. Among the earliest ministers for whom records exist were those who served 4,500 years ago in the court of Emperor Shun. Kao Yao was Shun's minister of justice. K'uei was his minister of music.

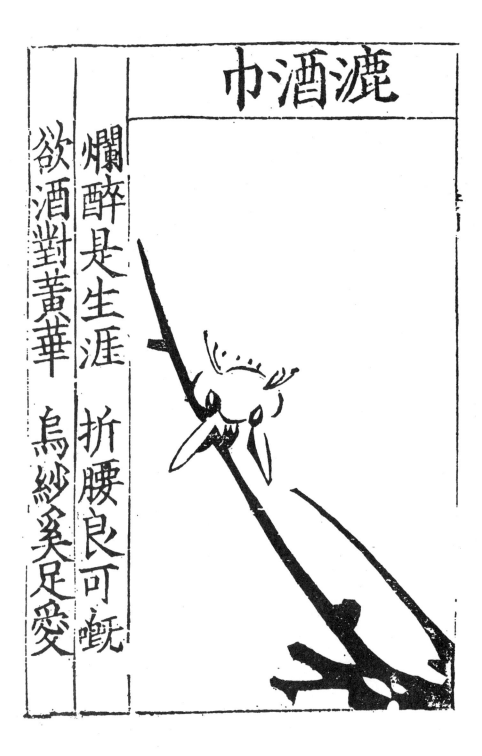

漉酒巾

爛醉是生涯　折腰良可㱇
欲酒對黃華　烏紗奚足愛

80. Wine-Straining Bandanna

falling down drunk is the life for me
bowing at the waist is depressing
I'd rather face yellow flowers with wine
a black silk hat is no concern of mine

The "yellow flowers" of the chrysanthemum are infused in hot water as well as in alcohol. It was the favorite flower of the poet T'ao Yuan-ming (365–427), who was known for his love of wine as well as for his disdain of official position. Chinese officials and members of the gentry were rarely without some sort of head covering. A hat of black silk was customary for officials carrying out their normal duties, while a simple bandanna was worn by peasants or people of modest means. T'ao Yuan-ming was known to take off his bandanna to strain wine, after which he then wrung it out and wrapped it back around his head.

抱葉蟬

槐柳午陰濃　淒涼聲愈健
欽露已成仙　軼雲齊女怨

81. Cicada Clinging to a Leaf

as willows and locusts turn dark at noon
its lonely chant grows stronger
drinking dew among the immortals
who says the Queen of Ch'i is displeased

The willow and the locust are two of the most common shade trees in China. In the third century B.C., the state of Ch'in was able to convince the King of Ch'i not to join a coalition against it. As a result, Ch'in was able to defeat the other states, including Ch'i, and unite all of China under its rule. The King of Ch'i's wife was so pained by her husband's blindness to Ch'in's intentions that she died of vexation and is said to have turned into a cicada, which Sung suggests may have been to her advantage. The cicada is an emblem of immortality, and the Chinese often place its jade likeness in the mouths of loved ones prior to burial. Rising out of the earth in spring and shedding its exuviae, it spends its summer afternoons in concert with other cicadas before returning to the earth in fall for another transformation. Dew is the drink of immortals, although wine is a close second.

穿花蝶

一夢在人間　東風吹不竟

莊周鴻冥冥　胡戀花枝巧

82. Butterfly among Flowers

it dreamed it was human once
and the east wind blew in vain
but while Chuang-tzu floated in the dark
what led him to this flowering branch

The east wind brings profit and fame, and it is rare for humans
not to be affected by it. Chuang-tzu relates how he once
dreamed he was a butterfly fluttering among flowers. But
when he awoke, he didn't know if he had dreamed he was a
butterfly, or if he were a butterfly dreaming he was Chuang-
tzu (*Chuangtzu:* 2). Here, Sung takes the latter view, of the
butterfly dreaming it is Chuang-tzu, a Chuang-tzu unaffected
by profit and fame and yet unable to escape the attraction
of beauty.

暮雀投林

倦翼已知還　投林謀夜宿
弋宿無容心　機深未爲福

83. Flying to the Woods at Dusk

weary wings know the way home
returning to the woods at night
to shoot a roosting bird is heartless
such cunning brings no blessing

Of Confucius it was said that he fished but never used a net,
that he hunted but never shot a roosting bird (*Analects: 7.26*).

寒鳥倚樹

人好鳥亦好　寒枝不輕踏
月明如可依　飛繞猶三匝

84. Crow Landing on a Tree in Winter

this applies to men or crows
view an icy branch with care
the moon is bright and rest is welcome
but still it circles a tree three times

In one of his "Short Ballads," Emperor Wu of the Wei dynasty wrote, "The moon is bright, stars are few / crows and magpies flying south / looking for a branch to rest on / circle trees three times." The crow's care in choosing a branch refers to a gentleman's care in choosing a lord to serve.

舞袖

舞劇更宜長　十筝藏纖指

脫得戲衫時　方知有獸底

85. Dancer's Sleeves

longer is better for dancing
and bamboo extensions hide small fingers
but when she takes her costume off
then we see how short they are

In traditional Chinese dance, long sleeves are swirled around
like huge ribbons by means of bamboo extensions attached to
the dancer's fingers. But officials at court also wore robes with
huge sleeves. Hence, Sung's reference here is to those whose
outward appearance belies their true form.

絲絲共白　歷遍風霜、

君王豈輕剪　欲療將軍安

86. Twirling Whiskers

whiskers whiskers all turned white
the border wind blows cold
kings don't lightly cut their beards
except to restore a general's health

The Chinese esteem beards, as they are signs of old age and long life. Hence, cutting them is considered unlucky as well as disrespectful toward one's parents and ancestors. However, once when a T'ang dynasty general became seriously ill, one of the emperor's advisers said he had heard that beard ashes were an effective cure. The emperor was so concerned about his general's health that he cut his own beard to prepare the medicine. Later, when the general recovered and tried to thank the emperor, the emperor said his action wasn't for the general's sake but for the country's.

鶯擲柳

金梭抛罷絲　東風弄晴晝
求友不須鳴　綠窗人倦繡

87. Oriole Flying through Willows

a golden shuttle crisscrosses kingfisher silk
the east wind brings clear skies
don't bother singing in search of a mate
behind the green screen she has given up weaving

The oriole and the willow are both symbols of spring, as is
the east wind. Here, the oriole also appears in this scene as
the golden shuttle and represents a young man in search of
his lover, while the kingfisher blue-green window screen,
conjured out of hanging willow catkins, signifies the room of
an unmarried woman of modest means. The third line is
paraphrased from "Cutting Down Trees" in the *Book of Songs,*
where birds find mates by singing. And the last line recalls a
poem by Pai Chu-yi in which a woman gives up waiting for
her lover and stops weaving, which was considered a woman's
lifelong duty—unless she did not marry.

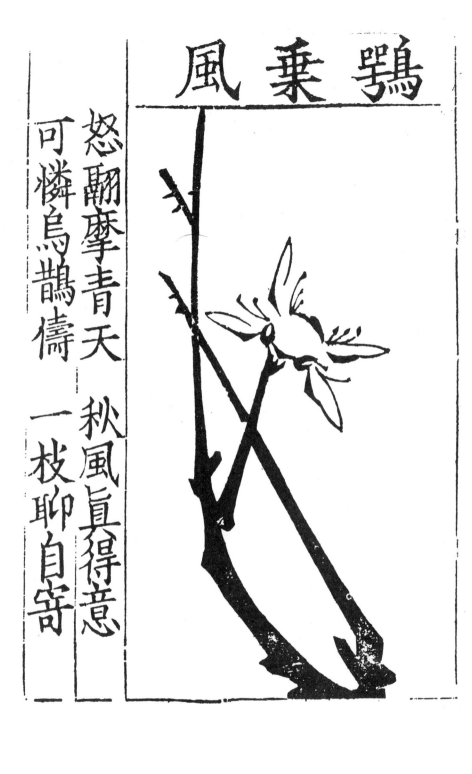

風乘鵶

怒翮摩青天

可憐烏鵲儔

秋風真得意

一枝聊自寄

88. Osprey Riding the Wind

wings outstretched against the blue
the autumn wind is perfect
pitiful crows and magpies
settle for a single branch

Chuang-tzu likens greater and lesser knowledge to a huge bird whose wings fill the sky and a small bird that makes do with a single branch (*Chuangtzu*: 1). The crows and magpies here refer to black-robed officials.

頂雪

滕六兩天花　南枝香鬬白

瓊玉兩模糊　冷笑從君索

89. Snowcap

T'ai-liu's falling celestial flowers
compete with a scented branch of white
indistinct from the purest jade
both elicit our icy laughter

T'ai-liu is the snow god, and the petal-like flakes he scatters
are said to rival those of the plum. The term "icy laughter"
normally refers to sarcasm, but here simply refers to the cold.
This also brings to mind the following pair of poems by
another Sung dynasty poet, Lu Mei-p'o, titled "The Snow
and the Plum." One: "The plum and the snow both claim
the spring / a poet gives up trying to decide / the plum must
admit the snow is three times whiter / but the snow can't
match a wisp of plum perfume." Two: "The plum without
the snow isn't very special / and snow without a poem is
simply commonplace / at sunset when the poem is done
then it snows again / together with the plum they complete
the spring."

風歌

暗香從何來　寒颷為輕扇

東君湏護持　莫點宮粧面

90. Windblown

where does that hidden scent come from
wafted here by a winter gale
may the Lord of the East protect it
keep it from gracing palace faces

The phrase "hidden scent" is another name for the plum blossom and recalls Lin Pu's famous couplet written at his hermitage in Hangchou in the eleventh century: "its hidden fragrance rides the wind / as the moon shines through the mist." The Lord of the East refers to the sun, the ruler of spring, at whose impending approach the plum surprises the winter landscape with its bloom. In addition to powder and paint, palace ladies also decorated their faces with moistened flower petals, a custom that some say began with Yang Kuei-fei (719–756).

蜻蜓欲立

四疊薄於紗　纖塵不相著
只在鈎絲邊　漁翁素盟約

91. Dragonfly Landing

two pairs of wings thinner than gauze
unmarked by the slightest dust
it perches upon a silken line
with the fisherman's agreement

This poem recalls Tu Fu's "Visiting the Ho Family Home Again," where the dragonfly's license to perch on a fisherman's line represents the familiarity that comes with a long-standing relationship. "Dust" refers to the world of sensation.

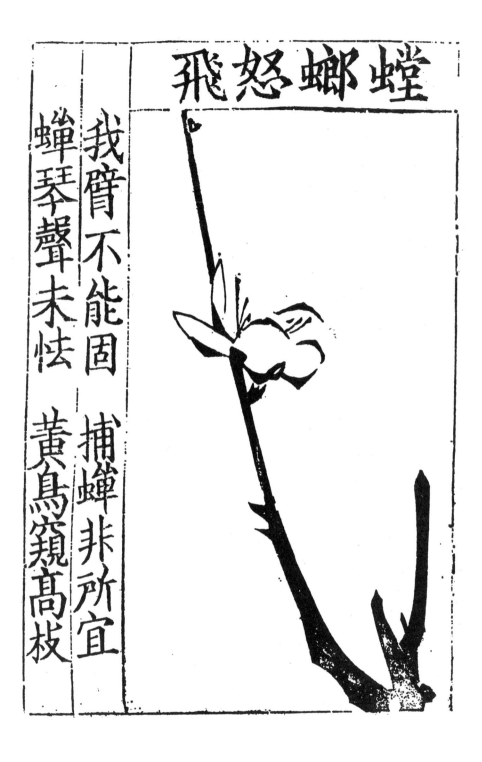

飛怒螳螳

我臂不能固　捕蟬非所宜

蟬琴聲未怯　黃鳥窺高枝

92. Mantis Trying to Fly

its arms aren't strong enough
and catching a cicada isn't safe
the cicada meanwhile sings without fear
but overhead an oriole watches

Among Chuang-tzu's stories is one in which a mantis trying
to stop a cart represents a person's unrealistic assessment of
his abilities (*Chuangtzu:* 4). In another, he recounts how a
mantis was once preparing to grab an unwitting cicada, and
this reminds him of a king who rushed to attack a neighbor-
ing state without bothering about the consequences. The
cicada, it turns out, was about to be grabbed by a bird, and
the bird was about to be shot by Chuang-tzu, who was about
to be arrested for poaching in the royal hunting preserve
(*Chuangtzu:* 20).

喜鵲搖枝

天上會雙星　橋渡銀河水
一別動經年　搓搓徒報喜

93. Magpie Rocking on a Branch

in the sky where two stars meet
a bridge spans the Silver River
another year since they parted
twitter twitter idle news

According to an ancient Chinese legend, the Sun married his daughter, Vega, to the Herdboy, Altair, in hopes that she would find an interest in life other than weaving. Unfortunately, his daughter became so enamored of her new lover that she gave up weaving altogether. This enraged the Sun so much, he ordered the couple to live on opposite shores of the Silver River, or Milky Way, except for one night a year, the seventh night of the seventh moon. On this night, all the magpies on Earth form a bridge on which the two lovers meet. The Chinese still celebrate this as Lover's Night.

水吹魚遊

春透水波明　江湖從落魄

三十六鱗成　禹門看一躍

94. Fish Spitting Water

spring skies are bright and the current is clear
vagabond soul of rivers and lakes
a perfect thirty-six scales
leap through Yu Gate in one try

The Yellow River is famous for its carp, which the Chinese also call "thirty-six scales" after a line of thirty-six black scales along the fish's flank. Yumen, or Yu Gate, is a narrow opening in the middle reaches of the river named after Yu the Great, who built his capital nearby in Linfen and who first brought the flooding of the Yellow River under control 4,200 years ago. When the Yellow River's water level recedes in winter, rapids appear at Yu Gate, and carp work their way with difficulty the following spring to their ancient spawning ground upstream. The chance of passing the civil service exams and gaining an official appointment was likened to that of a carp getting through this section of the river.

Forming Fruit

SIX BRANCHES

橘中四皓

就實四枝

羽翼漢家了 志形天地間
簡中有真樂 奚必拘商山

95. Four Worthies of Chungnan

lending support to the House of Han
forgetting the world in the world
in this there is true joy
why remain on Mount Shang

At the end of the third century B.C., four white-haired men
of integrity refused to serve the oppressive First Emperor of
the Ch'in dynasty and retired to Mount Shang on the south-
ern slopes of the Chungnan Mountains south of the capital of
Hsienyang. After the Han dynasty replaced the Ch'in,
Emperor Kao-tsu was on the point of replacing the crown
prince until these four sages left the mountains and came to
the boy's aid. In this poem Sung reveals a goal he shared with
other Confucian intellectuals: to transcend the world while
living in the world. In the 1261 edition of this book, the section
title, reproduced here, mistakenly reads "Four Branches"
instead of "Six Branches." The mistake was corrected in
subsequent editions.

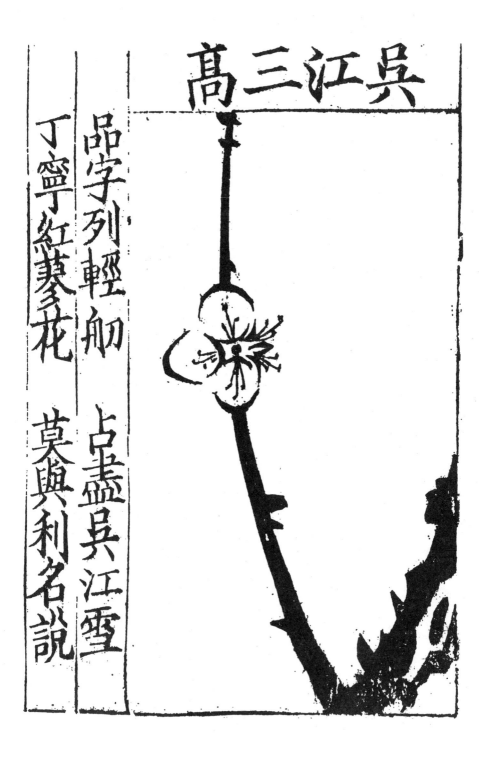

品字列輕舠　占盡吳江雪

丁寧紅蓼花　莫與利名說

96. Three High-Minded Men of Wuchiang

p'in connects three floating tubs
foretelling an end to Wuchiang snow
remember the red smartweed flower
don't talk about profit or fame

When the plum blossom is down to three petals, it resembles the Chinese character *p'in,* which reminds Sung of three tubs of the kind used to gather water caltrop in summer. "Wuchiang" is a name for the area along either side of the Yangtze near its mouth and is still known for its water caltrop. Three men who became recluses in this region included Fan Li in the fifth century B.C., Chang Han in the fourth century A.D., and Lu Kuei-meng in the eighth century. All three placed great emphasis on personal integrity, which is among the meanings of *p'in*. Seeing the flower down to three petals also reminds Sung that winter is over. Smartweed is distinguished by its sprays of rust-colored flowers and grows along China's waterways, where its wild habitat and somewhat bitter flavor have led to its association with hardship and the eremitic life.

二 疎

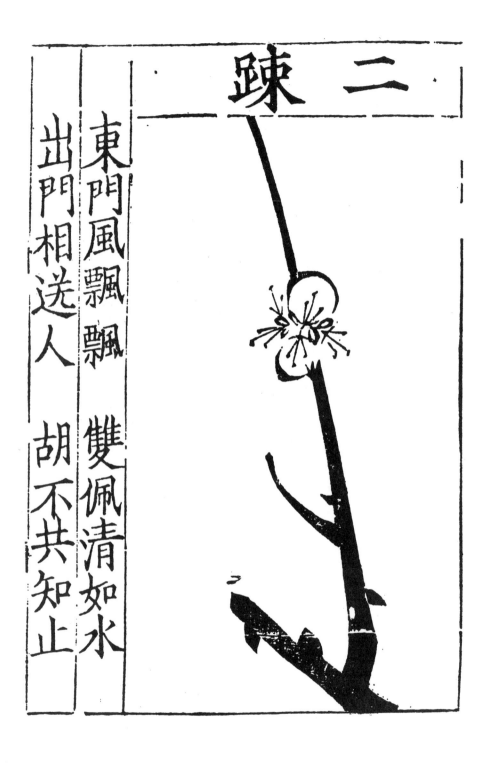

東門風飄飄　雙佩清如水
出門相送人　胡不共知止

97. Two Shus

two pendants pure as water
sway in the East Gate wind
why did those who saw them off
not share their sense of restraint

Shu Kuang and his nephew Shu Shou served as senior and
junior tutors to the crown prince during the reign of
Emperor Hsuan in the first century B.C. After the crown
prince ascended the throne as Emperor Yuan (B.C. 73–48),
they decided to retire to the countryside with their reputa-
tions intact, represented by the simple, pure white pendants
they wore at their waists, and here by the two white petals in
the woodblock print. Such was the esteem in which they were
held, all the officials in Ch'ang-an came to see them off at the
capital's East Gate. Many Chinese historians view Emperor
Yuan's reign as the beginning of the Han dynasty's decline.
Lao-tzu says, "who knows contentment / thus suffers no
shame / and who knows restraint / encounters no trouble /
while enjoying a long life" (*Taoteching*: 44). Again, Sung
criticizes the pursuit of wealth and power by his fellow
officials and sighs at their inability to know when to stop.

獨釣

一竿風雨寒　　獨占巖陵瀨

苟非伸脚眠　　曷見光武大

98. Fishing Alone

living apart at Yenling Bend
fishing in the cold windblown rain
sleeping with his feet stretched out
he showed us Kuang-wu's stature

Yen Tzu-ling lived in the first century A.D. and spent his days fishing from a rock that still bears his name along an especially scenic stretch of the Fuchun River south of Hangchou. He was once visited there by his boyhood companion, who had since restored the Han dynasty and ascended the throne as Emperor Kuang-wu. Unimpressed with his friend's attainments, Yen stretched out and fell asleep with his feet on the emperor's stomach. The incident did much to immortalize Kuang-wu as a tolerant ruler, and, no doubt, Sung is hoping for the same from his.

孟嘉落帽

醉帽不輕飛　秋菊有佳色
自慚群座中　主人猶未識

99. Meng Chia's Falling Cap

this drunk's cap doesn't fall without reason
the autumn mums are lovely
how sad among the guests
the host still doesn't know him

Meng Chia lived in the fourth century and was drinking with a group of officials the ninth night of the ninth moon, the night chrysanthemums are celebrated, when his cap blew off. The host noticed that Meng continued drinking as if nothing had happened. When Meng left briefly to relieve himself, the host asked someone to compose a poem making fun of the cap. When Meng returned and found his cap and a poem waiting for him, he replied with a poem of his own that earned him universal acclaim. About ten years earlier, a famous judge of men had been able to pick Meng out from a crowd of officials based purely on his reputation. Sung's second line is from one of T'ao Yuan-ming's "Drinking Poems" that was itself inspired by a line by Ch'u Yuan (d. 268 B.C.) about eating the fallen petals of chrysanthemums. Meng Chia was T'ao's maternal grandfather, and Sung's first two lines refer to their fortuitous connection. Sung's last two lines also refer to the failure of earlier rulers to recognize the talents of Ch'u and T'ao and, naturally, are meant to extend to himself as well.

商鼎催羹

脱白弄青玉　風味猶辛酸催

指日夢惟肖　羹調天下安卷終

100. Of Tripods and Soup

white replaced by greenest jade
a flavor truly sour
all too soon it's like a dream
the soup is seasoned the world at peace

The Chinese tripod that played such an important role in
court rituals was first used as a cooking pot. The sour green
fruit that replaces a plum's white blossom is also used as a
condiment in cooking. Presenting metaphors for good
government, the *Book of Documents* says, "Be my salt and
plums in seasoning the soup" (4.8).

ABOUT THE TRANSLATOR

Bill Porter assumes the pen name Red Pine for his translations. He was born in Los Angeles in 1943, grew up in the Idaho Panhandle, served a tour of duty in the U.S. Army (1964–67), graduated from the University of California–Santa Barbara with a degree in anthropology in 1970, and attended graduate school at Columbia University. Uninspired by the prospect of an academic career, he dropped out of Columbia in 1972 and moved to a Buddhist monastery in Taiwan. After four years with the monks and nuns, he struck out on his own and eventually found work at English-language radio stations in Taiwan and Hong Kong, where he produced over a thousand programs about his travels in China. In 1993 he returned to America with his family and has lived ever since in Port Townsend, Washington. His most recent publications include *Zen Baggage,* an account of a pilgrimage to sites associated with the beginning of Zen in China, and *In Such Hard Times,* a translation of the poetry of Wei Ying-wu, one of China's greatest poets.

Since 1972, Copper Canyon Press has fostered the work of emerging, established, and world-renowned poets for an expanding audience. The Press thrives with the generous patronage of readers, writers, booksellers, librarians, teachers, students, and funders—everyone who shares the belief that poetry is vital to language and living.

MAJOR SUPPORT HAS BEEN PROVIDED BY:

The Paul G. Allen Family Foundation

Amazon.com

Anonymous

Arcadia Fund

Diana and Jay Broze

Beroz Ferrell & The Point, LLC

Golden Lasso, LLC

Gull Industries, Inc.
on behalf of William and Ruth True

Lannan Foundation

Rhoady and Jeanne Marie Lee

National Endowment for the Arts

New Mexico Community Foundation

Cynthia Lovelace Sears and Frank Buxton

Washington State Arts Commission

Charles and Barbara Wright

To learn more about underwriting Copper Canyon Press titles,
please call 360-385-4925 ext. 103

The Chinese character for poetry is made up of two parts: "word" and "temple." It also serves as pressmark for Copper Canyon Press.

This book is set in Minion, designed for digital composition by Robert Slimbach in 1989. Minion is a neohumanist face, a contemporary typeface retaining elements of the pen-drawn letterforms developed during the Renaissance. Poems and display type are set in Classica, designed by Thierry Puyfoulhoux. Book design and composition by Valerie Brewster, Scribe Typography. Printed on archival-quality paper at McNaughton Gunn, Inc.